FOREWORD BY BOB BUFORD

Small Shifts in Leadership That Make a Big Difference

ERIK REES   JEFF JERNIGAN

ABINGDON PRESS / *Nashville*

TILT
SMALL SHIFTS IN LEADERSHIP THAT MAKE A BIG DIFFERENCE

Library of Congress Cataloging-in-Publication Data

Rees, Erik
  Tilt : small shifts in leadership that make a big difference / Erik Rees
and Jeff Jernigan.
    p. cm.
ISBN 978-1-4267-0579-3 (pbk. : alk. paper)
  1. Christian leadership. I. Jernigan, Jeff. II. Title.
  BV652.1.R445 2010
  253—dc22

2009049224

To
all pastors and leaders who strive every day
to fulfill their calling as servants and shepherds.
May God bless your life and your leadership beyond
your wildest dreams!
—Erik Rees

For Daniel,
a hero who always leads from the tilt.
—Jeff Jernigan

Contents

PART III: SUSTAINING YOUR LEADERSHIP

Foreword

Erik Rees and Jeff Jernigan have written a practical book that can have a dramatic impact on the lives and careers of ministry leaders. Twenty-five years ago when I began Leadership Network, a ministry to large church leaders, there were very few of what are now called megachurches (defined at that time as churches with a thousand or more attending). Today there are more than five thousand megachurches (with two thousand or more attending). That's quite a growth rate for an organization that used to be considered small and inflexible.

What changed? Giving full credit to the Father, Son, and Holy Spirit, my observation is that the main reason for this remarkable metamorphosis to large organizations, perhaps the major change since the Reformation's abandonment from hierarchical rule, has been a change in the work of leadership. Many churches haven't changed their leadership style at all; they are still small and denominational, and the work is expected to be done by the pastor—not much different really from the Jane Austen days.

Most of the small-church pastors are doers. Burnout rates are high. Management experts call these jobs "widow makers." That definition is applied when a job defeats two or three reasonably competent men. Their congregations are aging, their numbers are shrinking. Church historian Rodney Stark, in his latest book, documents dramatic decline in (mostly small and single-pastor) mainline churches (*What Americans Really Believe* [Waco, Texas: Baylor University Press, 2008], 22). For example, between 1960 and 2000, in terms of members per 1,000 U.S. population, the Episcopal Church declined 55 percent, The United Methodist Church declined 49 percent, and the Presbyterian Church (USA) declined 49 percent.

The big change in the ever-growing megachurches has been that senior pastors have learned to be leaders more than doers. They have learned to release and direct the energy of their large staffs and their corps of volunteers to do the work of the church. Increasingly, they have been instrumental in releasing the energy of laypeople to serve as what I call "Social Entrepreneurs" outside the four walls of the churches to transform communities. For example, sixty-three churches that participated for two years in Leadership Network's Innovative Practice Leadership Community for Externally Focused Churches increased the total number of hours served in community projects by 191 percent in two years—a total of 2,029,153 hours in 2008. And the churches learned to do it from one another.

Rick Warren and I both had the great good fortune of being mentored by Peter Drucker, often called "the Father of Modern Management." Peter focused an increasing amount of attention on what he called the "Social Sector" in the last twenty-five years of his long career. The megachurch was Peter's last great organizational discovery before his death at age ninety-five in 2005. He was quoted in *Forbes* magazine as saying "The emergence of the large pastoral church is the most significant social event of the last thirty years of the twentieth century." In 1991, Peter told me my mission was "to work on transforming the latent energy in American Christianity into active energy." That transformation was a major result of Saddleback Church and the many other megachurches that Rick Warren and Erik Rees have influenced in their work together. That's what this fresh new book is about. I call it the "Release Movement." Erik and Jeff have captured well the spirit of release.

Bob Buford
Founder, Leadership Network
www.leadnet.org

Acknowledgments

I want to thank God for allowing me to serve him as a leader at Saddleback Church. I'm humbled and honored to be used in the roles you grant me. I want to thank Rick Warren for constantly believing in me and challenging me to create new models of ministry. I want to thank those who have walked ahead of me and developed ways to equip and empower the body of Christ. I fully realize I'm standing on your great foundation of work. Last, I want to thank my wife, Stacey, for continually cheering for me as a husband, father, author, and leader.

—Erik Rees

Without someone committed to acquisition who understands their business and the marketplace, a good book can remain an imaginative fancy; never seeing print, never impacting lives or changing ministries. Thank you, Jessica Kelley, for your interest in this work. Without an editor the mistakes, ellipses, hyperbole, and confused ideation will not be corrected, smoothed, and put in a language the reader can understand and enjoy so that all those dreams an author has—and is convinced cannot be improved upon—will reach an audience. Thank you, John Kutsko, for your partnership in the process. Thank you as well to the Abingdon team. We know you are there, invisible, making the wheels turn in the machinery of publishing, pumping clarity into every product. Of course, there is the agent as well . . . managing authors with strong opinions, interpreting author-speak for the publisher, guiding the process to its satisfactory conclusion. Thank you, Nancy, for what you do and who you are. There are so many to thank who contributed to this book through the testimony of their struggles and successes in life and ministry. For all of you who were and are unintentional collaborators, we are grateful.

—Jeff Jernigan

Introduction

A simple tilt can transform something ordinary and common-place, something well understood and familiar, into a powerful and unalterably different force. Just a simple tilt, a shifting of perspective, a change in approach, and everything suddenly takes on new meaning.

The edge of a kite tilting into the wind can send it soaring. The rudder tilted just a few inches more throws the entire vessel hard over into a bone-crushing turn, gaining a valuable and irre-placeable length on the boat next to you. Tilt the umbrella just a little more, and you've sheltered a loved one from the blowing rain. Tilt your gaze just slightly, and the picture hidden behind all the specks of color suddenly comes to life. Tilting can bring energy to the complacent, victory to the loser, comfort to the weary, and animation to the lifeless.

If we are to create hope for those in ministry who earnestly desire to take things to a higher level, to experience success they never imagined, to leave fatigue and discouragement behind them, and to create new life in the kingdom—and empower others to join them in this great adventure—then we and they must learn to tilt.

Some of what you are about to discover will seem like new ground, and there are new perspectives and new tools to consider in these pages. However, all the basic parts you are familiar with and have been trained in and have practiced for years are all here as well. And then again, they are not. At least not in quite the same way you may have learned, understood, or applied. We take these simple truths and tilt them just a bit, discovering how this simple act has transformed so many people and so many ministries.

We have spent our entire careers discovering how to transform people and ministries by applying common truths in uncommon ways. Both of us have been successful corporate executives. Both are successful in ministry as pastors and missionaries. Both currently serve in ministry full-time in addition to speaking, publishing, counseling, and coaching others interested in looking at growth and change in life and ministry from a different perspective. Both discovered our passion and purpose as a result of a simple tilt: When you uncover God's design and calling in your life and identify God's specific purpose for you, life becomes an adventure!

Everything you do becomes nearly effortless; resistance seems to fade away. When you are operating in ministry according to your design, the days end with exhilaration, not depression. When those you serve alongside are fitted together based on their design, and all of you together are fitted to the calling of your ministry like a hand in a tailored glove, an explosion takes place. This element of design, when acknowledged and accommodated, is the tilt you bring to every dimension of ministry, transforming it forever.

We offer no promise of a problem-free future in ministry for you. In fact, we guarantee new challenges, new obstacles, as you adapt the ideas you find here to your situation. What we can assure you of is security in knowing that you are equipped to struggle well. Struggle is a central concept in transformation. In fact, the word often used for transformation or change in Scripture is *metamorphosis*, the same word we use to describe the process of larvae becoming beautiful butterflies. The very struggle of emerging from the cocoon is what guarantees the health, vigor, and ultimate success of the butterfly.

To help in this process, each chapter challenges you to think in new ways about yourself and about ministry, and includes a number of exercises to draw out your thoughts, letting you practice your tilt. You will also see callouts contrasting common leadership wisdom with a subtle twist on that wisdom—the tilt. The "common leadership wisdom" captures a truth. Each is true to some degree . . . just not as relevant or effective as another truth. The "tilt" captures a greater truth that is related to but very different from what common wisdom may suggest.

Along the way, we share our own failures and victories as well as those of others. In some cases we have changed the names of the people involved or altered the details of the circumstances in order to provide confidentiality. In most cases we communicate in the first person without reference to who is speaking, Erik or Jeff. Additional resources are appended and we are always available online at www.empoweringchurches.com. We are grateful for the opportunity to be a good read for you. It is our passion, our purpose, part of what we want to give away. We pray what you find here will give you new hope and be truly empowering.

> In gratitude for his grace,
> Erik Rees
> Jeff Jernigan

PART I

EMPOWERED TO LEAD

CHAPTER ONE

Becoming an Empowering Leader

I pray that from his glorious, unlimited resources he will empower you with inner strength through his Spirit. Then Christ will make his home in your hearts as you trust in him. Your roots will grow down into God's love and keep you strong. —Ephesians 3:16-17 NLT

How willing are you to be honest about what really counts when it comes to success in ministry? If it were possible to identify with certainty the kind of leader you wanted to be, know you can be, and know that God has gifted you to be, would you be willing to ask the question? God has a game plan for each of us, and he is waiting to pour that game plan into us the moment we are honestly ready for answers.

Here is a secret: You already know the answers. They have been part of your design from the very beginning.

Like many committed people in ministry, I have fallen prey to the Mr. Potato Head syndrome. My experiences speaking, consulting, and ministering around the world have a common thread running through them. We have all the pieces to the puzzle already. In fact, all the pieces are in one box; but, like Mr. Potato Head, they have not been put together in the right places.

The concepts and principles in this book will help you find new passion, new purpose, and new ideas to help you grow your ministry and so fulfill God's plan for your life. You will discover and assemble all the pieces. Imagine the power to be released as you help others discover and fulfill their God-given strengths for service!

When your purpose breaks upon you with the clarity of a new vision, and you seize your purpose as the kind of leader God has designed and called you to be; your church, your ministry, whatever it happens to be, will forever be changed.

It starts with simply wanting to know God's plan, discovering his purpose for your life as a leader, and trusting God for the results. And what a wonderful companion we have on this journey of discovery! Jesus will reveal himself to us (John 14:21) and through his Spirit living in us, he will teach us all that we need to know (John 14:26).

I love to run. Competing in a race totally energizes me, and what I really enjoy is a long-distance run. It challenges me physically, mentally—even spiritually—as nothing else does. It reminds me, too, of what ministry can be like. A lot of us in ministry can relate to the marathon runner. Marathon runners will tell you there's a point in the race, somewhere about the two-thirds mark, where they "hit the wall." Their physical endurance has been pushed to the limit. Their brain is telling their body it just can't go on—and their spirit is starting to listen. When a marathon runner is completely exhausted and there are still five or six miles to go, he finds out what he's really made of.

Maybe you're there right now. Your church or ministry isn't growing and you are completely exhausted. Physically, you are on the verge of burnout. Mentally, you are out of ideas. Spiritually, you are about to give up. All of us have been there at one time or another. And those who haven't will be there sooner or later. It's like running in place: Your legs are pumping but you're not getting anywhere.

Whether you are in that place of exhaustion now—ready to give up on your ministry—or you are looking to prevent a burnout you see headed your way, you are to be applauded for being proactive. Your reading choice says a lot about you and your desire to become the leader God created you to be.

You certainly are not alone. A recent study I conducted of more than one thousand church leaders found that 57 percent of them didn't have an avenue in ministry to express their God-given strengths and passions on a weekly basis. That news crushes my heart! This misalignment of design and duties leaves leaders feeling frustrated and fatigued rather than fulfilled and fruitful, which is what God desires for all of us to experience in our ministries. This book, first and foremost, is about finishing your race well, in victory!

Our desire is that God will give you the confidence to share your new ministry with those you lead. Through them God will move your ministry into a future far greater than you have imagined, even in your wildest dreams!

Training for the Race

One of the most empowering aspects of serving at Saddleback Church is that Pastor Rick Warren does not just tell us what we should do—he leads the way. He shows us how to release our members into ministry by setting the example. By motivating his staff in this way, Rick lets us know that we—and I—must also model this to our teams so they will follow our lead as we follow Rick's.

Who is the Rick Warren in your life? Who inspires you to want to be like him or her and in so doing look a little more like Jesus? Finding and focusing on a mentor to model your life after could be just the second wind you need to finish this marathon race called your ministry.

A mentor, intentional or unintentional, may be something you want to add to your personal development. Let's talk about what to *subtract* from what you do for a moment.

A principal reason many church leaders are not maximizing their strengths and passion is that *they are doing too much*. Admit it; many of us have serious control issues. One pastor said to me, "Erik, I would *rather* do it all."

"If you try to do it all," I told him, "you will end up doing nothing."

Do you see a wick coming out of your head or your feet? God didn't design us to burn the candle at both ends. Rather, the Bible calls church leaders to *share* their ministry, so the church can reach its full potential.

If you are one of those who want to do it all, you are in good company. Most church leaders I work with have some level of control issues. If they deny it, that's a good sign they are wrong.

Rick Warren told me about his experience of trying to do it all back when he was a young pastor. One day he woke up and found himself in a serious state of depression. It was there that God got hold of his heart and showed him his job was *not* to do it all, but to empower those he led to play their part. That way—and only that way—everything that needs doing can get done.

I admit it: I struggle with control issues in my life and ministry. (Just ask my wife!) I have a long way to go! My confession today as a broken man is that God is the hero of everything I do.

When God called me out of corporate America to join the Saddleback Church staff, my control issues were at an all-time high. I was used to doing everything by myself and for myself— but Saddleback Church did not operate that way. Over and over, Rick would pull me aside and say, "Erik, only you can be you, so let go and let God lead."

Today I see that embracing his sage advice was the first time I was asked to "tilt" my life and my leadership style. We explored the concept of a "servant leader," the idea that I didn't have to make it happen in order to get things done, the revolutionary thought that I should "let go" in order to provide *more* direction, and the reality that leadership is not just a skill but a quality of my character. It wasn't a complete overhaul—all the right ideas were there—but it sure was a different way of living them out! Having been taught these things over years of development, I thought I understood them; but I grew to realize that it was the words I understood and that true spiritual transformation is more than just mastering a vocabulary.

God used Rick to teach me some vital life and leadership lessons, all of which I share with you in this book. As God used him to teach me how to make God the hero of both my life and my leadership, I now want to pass those tips on to you. This is not about bragging, just sharing what has worked for me, what has kept me aligned with God's purpose, what has allowed God to work through me, and what can help you make it to the finish line standing up.

No matter where you are as a leader in ministry, you will benefit greatly from the journey ahead. Some of these benefits include: reduced stress, increased success, enhanced self-worth, boosted sense of significance, enlarged influence, strengthened staff/volunteers, and an expanded servant heart.

It's all about becoming the leader God designed you to be. This path has nothing to do with building a huge church; it has everything to do with honoring God with your leadership. Only by God's grace do we get to lead other people. As we lead people—and more important, as we accept them—God is glorified. The Bible says, "Therefore, accept each other just as Christ has accepted you so that God will be given glory" (Romans 15:7 NLT). So whether your ministry is to ten people or ten thousand, empowering people and glorifying God should always be your leadership goal.

Realignment

It is impossible to fully understand the masterpiece of your life if you are disconnected from the Creator, the master artist who sees you always as a masterpiece no matter where you are in the process of being conformed to his image. Anything that is slowing you down or distracting you from being everything God created you to be needs to be removed as an obstacle. What things in your life get in the way? Where are you distracted by ministry tasks that ought to belong to someone else in the church? Are there areas of your life that need to be surrendered to God?

Jonah is a great example of a spiritual leader in need of realignment. He had things going pretty well for himself when God came along and gave him new orders. Jonah was going to be the first prophet sent to a foreign nation. In some respects Jonah could have viewed this as a promotion, an exciting gig, a new opportunity to spread truth in unbelieving parts of the world. Only, there is a problem: Jonah has other plans. You know the story: Jonah runs the other way and gets into a whale of a problem.

By the end of the story Jonah comes to an important realization. He says to himself, "Those who regard vain idols forsake their faithfulness" (Jonah 2:8 NASB). In context, the vain idol Jonah refers to is his own opinion and judgment regarding what he should be doing and the direction his ministry should be moving in. He is misaligned with God's purposes for his life—a calling he has been uniquely prepared for and positioned to carry out.

When I get distracted by my plan to the point that I no longer see God's plan, two things usually happen: My plan becomes an idol in the sense that it replaces in my life what God has called me to in that moment. Moreover, I become exhausted trying to make my plan work. God equips and empowers me for his work, and when I am misaligned that empowerment is no longer there. No wonder I end days worn out rather than energized!

Common Leadership Wisdom: We are empowered and equipped by God for the work of ministry.

The Tilt: We are the most empowered for ministry when we are in alignment with God's plans and not our own.

Just like getting our back realigned by a chiropractor or our car's wheels realigned by a mechanic, we must take the time to make sure we are totally aligned with God so he can give us the clarity and confidence to be who he made us to be and do what he desires us to do.

The amazing thing about an active lordship of Christ in your life is that you can see clearly what to seize, or take hold of, in the ministry he created you for! The Bible tells us that we were designed by God to make a difference for God. I truly hope that as you realign with God this "tilt" will empower you to see not only your unique design but also the specific difference he wants you to make in the world through your ministry.

Let yourself dream big for God's glory! Be ready to develop a core team of dedicated people around you to help make your kingdom dream come true! God will show you how to truly release his people to fulfill their purpose so the needs within the body of Christ can be met by the body of Christ. Notice that it is God releasing his people, not you releasing your people, for the exercise of their purpose in the body and not your purpose for them. As people are released into ministry, they will need help developing their strengths and passions. Simply put, you need to invest in them. At some point you will move away from equipping people to empowering them to fulfill their God-ordained purpose.

A Place to Begin

Before you begin, take a moment to mark your starting place. Where are you today, right now, at the beginning of your adventure with God?

After years of working with churches and ministries, watching their progress carefully, I have discovered that most organizations tend to land in one of four categories when it comes to releasing their members into volunteer service. The classification is determined largely by the degree to which they invite others to serve with them and the degree to which they strategically invest in the lives of these faithful servants.

First, there is the *Expressionless Ministry*. Leaders in this ministry expend little or no effort inviting others to serve and do not invest in those who may be serving already. There is virtually no expression of ministry from the body of Christ. The professionals are doing all the work and members are not being invited to serve in ministry. So they just watch while the paid staff does it all. Because the members have limited resources to even discover what their God-given strengths and passions are, there is little likelihood they will find their best place to serve God.

Then, there is the *Exhausted Ministry*. This ministry spends lots of time and resources inviting others to serve with them, but invests little time and energy in those who are serving. People are always being challenged: "Come on! Serve the Lord with me!" A lot of work gets done, but 20 percent of the people are trying to do 80 percent of the work. Some are trying to do too much, and others are serving in the wrong positions. Too much of this, and you can find yourself right back at Expressionless Ministry when the square pegs get tired of working in round holes, wear out, and go home. Because no one is investing in the people with training and support, they get fatigued and frustrated, rather than feeling fulfilled and fruitful.

If you are successful at developing volunteers to understand their strengths and passions, you may find yourself working in an *Equipped Ministry*. This ministry spends a lot of time investing in people, but seldom invites them to serve. It's like they are all dressed up for a big dance, but there's no ballroom! People in this ministry have all the tools and have practiced the skills, but have no opportunity to apply what they have learned. They understand God has uniquely made them for a mission. But few ministry opportunities are offered, and what is offered doesn't tap into their individual strengths and passions, or fit them together as a team.

Finally, there is the released ministry, or *Empowering Ministry*. This ministry constantly invites people to serve in a wide variety of ways while maintaining a high level of investing. The people involved are excited about serving God in ministry through their strengths and passions. They experience great significance, satisfaction, and success. This can happen only if a place has been made for the members. If no current opportunity taps into their God-given strengths and passions, they are given permission to start something new.

Ministry Matrix

Use the following matrix to determine where your church is currently. This will help you determine your starting point as you look to tilt your ministry toward building an empowering culture of ministry.

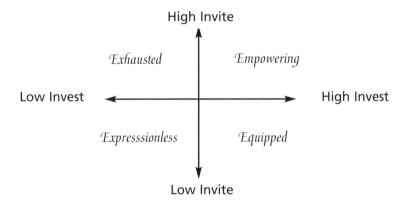

These four categories do not represent anything new on the frontier of ministry growth. But here is the "tilt": Progressing your ministry from Expressionless to Equipped begins with reproducing your ministry in others, so that they are empowered to lead and serve as well.

Leadership includes reproducing yourself in others. This helps avoid the Expressionless Ministry by getting others on board with the work of serving. Reproducing yourself in others includes helping others discover what they are best at doing; what they are

> **Common Leadership Wisdom:** Leadership aims for your followers *to implement your directions.*
>
> **The Tilt:** Leadership aims for your followers *to reproduce your heart, vision, and know-how.*

gifted and called to do. Working out of their area of giftedness helps avoid the burnout characterizing an Exhausted Ministry and provides the training people need for an Equipped Ministry. Having thought through what opportunities are available to serve, and even having a process identified to respond to fresh new Spirit-led opportunities for ministry, helps take men and women beyond an Equipped Ministry and release them into an Empowering Ministry. Here is the movement we want to encourage in the development of your ministry:

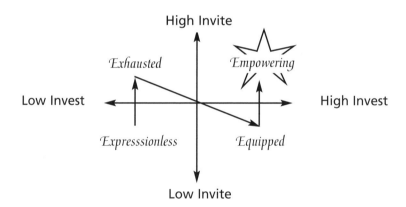

The idea of identifying gifts, calling, design, and purpose, and then organizing people together around their best fit in ministry while at the same time thinking ahead to what reasonable opportunities may give this ministry expression—well, that is leading-edge! So, how would you characterize your ministry? Mark the statements below that you believe are most descriptive of the ministry you are involved in right now.

Evaluate Your Ministry

Control (who makes decisions)
1. All decisions go through the senior staff leader.
2. All decisions go through a few key people or groups.
3. All decisions go through the appropriate ministry teams.
4. All decisions involve stakeholders appropriately.

Bench (who does the work)
1. There is little training or development of leadership.
2. There are few ministry leaders outside the paid staff.
3. Some ministry leaders are intentionally trained, but not all.
4. A program exists for developing leaders at all levels.

Volunteers (how volunteers are prepared and utilized)
1. Most of the work of ministry is carried out by paid staff.
2. Volunteers are plugged in wherever there is a need.
3. Volunteers are organized and equipped to serve.
4. Volunteers are utilized based on gifts, passion, and best fit.

Emphasis (the rationale behind your staffing decisions)
1. Focus is on covering the bases and getting things done.
2. Focus is on making sure all the ministries are staffed.
3. Focus is on participation and partnership in ministry.
4. Focus is on the contribution God calls you to make.

Which numbers collected the most check marks?

These styles correspond to the four categories of ministry we have just been talking about. If you had mostly ones, your ministry tends toward Expressionless. Mostly twos, Exhausted. Mostly threes, Equipped. Mostly fours, Empowering.

Where are you in each category? Ask yourself what needs to happen in order for you to move the ministry closer to what is described in option 4 under each category. This will help you identify actionable goals in moving toward an Empowering Ministry.

From *Tilt: Small Shifts in Leadership That Make a Big Difference* © 2010 by Erik Rees and Jeff Jernigan. Used by permission.

There Is Only One Answer

With more than fifty years of combined ministry experience serving church and missions organizations around the world ranging in size from 50, to 300, to 1,500, to 20,000-plus members, we can tell you that empowering ministry is not only possible, but necessary. If your ministry isn't empowering, you will eventually do harm to yourself and others.

A knock on the door introduced me one evening to a church that had been in existence for ten years but kept repeating the experiences of the first year over and over again. After ten years, all the staff could really say was that they had one year of experience and were suffocating under the weight of all that repetition. They had been ministering in the community for ten years and had progressed from expressionless to exhausted, and the pastor walked away burned out. Now they were in real trouble.

The ministry had no business plan or strategic ministry plan to guide their efforts. The church was a pastor-focused, family-run congregation struggling to get to a place where they could be a staff-run, elder-led body. There was no bench. Because decision making had been centralized in just a few, no one was ever given progressively more responsibility to develop their skill-set and faithfulness. Volunteers were snatched up and tossed into the fray wherever needed to serve until they burned out and another sacrifice was needed.

Key families left the ministry with the resulting financial pressure threatening to close the doors for good. Outreach in even the most basic forms of community service wasn't happening because the few volunteers not disgruntled, worn-out, or fed up were needed to staff the ministries still up and running. Leaderless, with no one *equipped* or *empowered*, the ministry was asphyxiating. A few families came that evening to ask us if we would consider helping them breathe some air back into the ministry. The rest is a success story that worked itself out over time as we led them through the series of tilts described in this book.

Most ministries don't find themselves in such desperate straits but can identify with some of these experiences. The question becomes: Do you see any room for change that may be an improvement in your own ministry? God's desire is for you to be completely sold on his vision, to see the masterpiece he wants to create out of your life and ministry. Moving on to what is next in this book is more than just turning a page. It is committing to inquiry, discovery, contemplation, evaluation, and best of all—implementation.

We begin with a frank look in the mirror. Actually, we will peer through the looking glass into our very souls where the seeds for success or sabotage have already been sown. If we cannot master our own motivation for ministry, all the tools in the world will not empower us to release others for ministry. Letting go is not the end of things; it is only the beginning.

CHAPTER TWO

The Empowering Pathway

You shall receive power when the Holy Spirit has come upon you; and
you shall be witnesses to Me in Jerusalem, and in all Judea and
Samaria, and to the end of the earth. —Acts 1:8 NKJV

We topped out just before the sun went down and managed to get all the gear up before the stars came out. Climbing thirty-five hundred vertical feet of the largest granite monolith in the world was giving us a moment of incredulity as we sat and lay about looking at the pinpoints of light like holes in the bottom of heaven shining down their congratulations. Our breath was a vapor puffing small clouds of steam like strange airborne bubbles in the stillness on top of the mountain at nearly eight thousand feet above sea level. We had conquered El Capitan.

Two years of hard work had been invested in the adventure of the last three days. Countless hours of reading, of physical training, of interviewing climbers who had been there and done that, and of practice climbs through every crux we could expect to encounter. So many plans made, worked through practically and then discarded, equipment checked and rechecked, handoffs and relays executed repetitively, sequenced leads and belays worked through hanging from climbing walls that we knew were far more forgiving than stone walls.

The focus it all required! Concentration, undistracted and unpolluted, became a mantra. How to cope with the exposure—not just to the elements, but emotionally—with the fear that would send your head spinning, beauty that would make your heart ache, and endurance that wouldn't quit. Mental toughness was the most difficult part of preparation because it comes by doing the real thing and not just by thinking about it.

We all made it. No injuries, everyone doing his or her part. Along the way we discovered empowerment. In fact, looking back it is clear now that we were all on a pathway of sorts that in the absence of deviation brought us to a place of deeply personal victory.

Ministry is like that as well, at least successful ministry. It takes preparation and practice, learning and processing, experimenting and failing. Eventually success comes as much as a fruit of hard work as it does of spiritual strength. There is a pathway that empowers for ministry. One that empowering leaders have experienced over and over again. The elements of this pathway are addressed throughout this book from the perspective of practical spirituality, acknowledging that building a house takes lots of tools and skills; yet it is far more than tools and skills. Our trust and faith must be focused on Christ since he alone is ultimately the builder of his house and we are the exquisite instruments of his craft.

The Apostle Peter was a real go-getter. He was ready for almost anything, and his willingness to jump in and make things happen often got him in trouble. In Matthew 4:19 Jesus finds him fishing and invites Peter to "follow Me, and I will make you [a fisher] of men" (NASB). At the end of the story in John 21:19 we find Jesus once more at the seashore with the disciples busy fishing. Jesus says again to Peter, "Follow Me!" (NASB). What happened in Peter's life in between those two invitations made the difference between a man bent

Common Leadership Wisdom: God calls us to be *builders of ministry.*

The Tilt: God calls us to be *the instruments of his building of the ministry.*

on doing things his own way and a servant leader committed to doing things God's way. It took frustration, fear, and failure, but Peter learned the difference between being the builder and being an instrument of the Builder. He tilted from trying to be a builder of the ministry to being an instrument of what God was building. Answering the call to "follow Me!" means I understand that there is someone other than me in the lead, someone else calling the shots and directing my efforts. Do I really believe because it is the sweat on my brow that I am the one getting all the work done? Or is it Jesus Christ working through me, empowering my efforts and anointing the results?

All of us tend to compartmentalize life and consequently easily separate building a ministry from building our relationship with Jesus Christ as though they are not the same thing. Sadly, if we are not intimately related to Christ, we may be successful in building a ministry, but it will not be his ministry.

We have discovered seven elements, steps, or phases along this pathway from being a builder of ministry to being an instrument in God's building of the ministry. Keep in mind that the empowering pathway has more to do with the outflow of your life than it does a formula for success. A pathway can be a course of action leading to a conclusion, a line of communication represented in telephone poles that connect your voice to my ear over great distances, a sequence of domino-like reactions, virtually anything that links elements together that move in a direction and arrive at a result. For those climbers it was joining a select group of people who have accomplished something really great. For you it means the same thing. Stay on this path and you will not only find empowerment, but you will join an elite group of difference makers in the kingdom of God who are accomplishing some very great things.

The pathway consists of seven elements: connection, clarification, contribution, collaboration, commission, comfort, and completion. More or less sequential, they all continue in some form once set in motion and you will revisit some more than once in your journey.

Connection

My wife is the finest person I know. I prefer her company over anyone else's. She is incredibly intelligent, successful, and gorgeous. She loves Jesus Christ, and what's more, she loves me! We talk often throughout every day. Even when I am several continents away we manage to find a way to connect each day. This has gone on for years and years. Our church staff speculates out loud that we are stuck in the teen years; but secretly, they are encouraged that their pastor and his wife are deeply in love and work at it every single day.

Do you have this kind of connection with God? It is the kind he wants! He so longs for prayer to be more for us than just our tool for self-expression. God wants a relationship, a best-friend connection. That doesn't happen without surrender. Surrender comes up a number of times in the following pages, both in practical how-tos and in taking you deeper. How much of what you do needs to be surrendered because it is about you and not Jesus? Looking back at more than three decades of ministry, I am surprised at how much of it was about me. Yes, God was in it all the time accomplishing his purposes. What could have been different if I had gotten myself out of the way?

" 'Call to Me, and I will answer you, and show you great and mighty things, which you do not know"; "Lift up your voice with strength, lift it up, be not afraid" (Jeremiah 33:3; Isaiah 40:9 NKJV). When is the last time you called on the Lord, really cried out to him? Did you know that the words for *joy, gratitude*, and *grace* were built from the same root in New Testament language? When we connect with God, the response in our hearts to his grace is one of joy and gratitude. When is the last time you felt that kind of energy in your prayer life? God wants us to cry out to him, not in some simpering whisper almost as if we were whiningly ashamed, but in strength and power—loudly, as if we had a right to demand an audience, a conversation, and a connection.

We talk a lot about connection in this book in many practical ways, often not even using the word. Look for it. Practice the practical in pursuit of the profound. The difference you have been designed and shaped to make in the kingdom begins with a connection.

Clarification

We cannot tell you how many times we have coached people we call "circumstantial dropouts." These are people who just bump along in life, letting circumstances dictate who they become without any consideration of what God has designed and called them to be. We have added lots of tools in this book to help you help others get on top of this issue—no worries there. Pause for a moment and consider the consequences if you don't. You—they—could become a Don.

Don enjoyed high school without really focusing on the future. He was bright enough to get decent grades and was in a college prep track that got him admitted to college. He didn't work too hard and his parents encouraged him to have fun. As long as he stayed out of trouble and got good grades he was off the radar screen as far as his counselors at school were concerned; nobody invested any time in developing his ambition or asking him to do hard things. He was a veteran dodger of hard things, cruising through life focused on fun and the easy way.

The fact that people throughout history had discovered new continents, and conquered them, advanced science and discovered calculus, among other things, by the time they were his age made no difference. He was still a self-absorbed, intellectually lazy, entitled teenager drifting along. In college he declared no major, took what classes were recommended, drank beer, and ate pizza with gusto, unconcerned about the future. If you asked him about dreams for the future, vision, or a sense of personal mission, you would have received the obligatory "Huh?"

When Don graduated from college he returned home to live with his parents, unsure of what he really wanted to do in life.

His mom welcomed the arrangement. Don was her little boy, the baby of the family, and she needed him to need her . . . you know the story. Don is unemployed and still living at home nearing forty years of age. True story, just not his real name. There are millions of Dons in the United States today. No clarity, no vision, no mission, no passion.

Now, if you are reading this book you are probably not a Don. We are not suggesting you take on all the Dons of the world, either. But you may be at a place or know others who are at a place in life where future direction needs clarification. What is your passion? What have you been called to? What are you best designed to do? What are your dreams and how can you best get on with living them out? We can help you answer those questions and then you can pass your knowledge on to those in your sphere of influence who could use the same encouragement. It is important at the outset that you are clear about what you are called to, what you are headed toward. At some point it will be that clarity alone that keeps you on the pathway.

Contribution

For many years I was Don-like in my career. Following the advice of my parents and school counselors, I pursued an education focused on what I seemed to have an aptitude for: things technical, science- and math-related, and jobs that used the high-tech stuff I was learning. It made sense, and it was fun in a novel kind of way for a while. I had the opportunity to invent things, to fly airplanes, to research some pretty sophisticated stuff, as well as play around with electricity. Because I had an aptitude for such things, I did well enough to be promoted to levels of higher responsibility. However, there came a time when I realized that just because someone might do something well doesn't mean that is what he or she has been designed to do.

I was pretty unhappy. Making factories run better, creating new radar systems, inventing products that can make torpedoes spin through the water at sixty miles per hour, punching holes in the sky with the newest airframes, and studying the transfer of heat across bimetal boundaries was drying me up inside like a plum gone prune. This is not what I was designed for and, more important, not what I was called to by the God who created in me a unique purpose.

The one thing about all those experiences that screamed loudly was a single common factor: The joy extracted from these tasks was the time spent with people, especially when it involved helping to make them healthier, wiser, or more successful. I was made for people, not tasks. What a phenomenal release I felt when it became clear to me that the contribution God wants from any of us is in the context of how he made us, and that in finding this place we can experience the "joy inexpressible" of the outcome of our faith (1 Peter 1:8 NKJV). Not only can we find our fit in ministry that maximizes our contribution, we can fit others together with us into a team that multiplies our contribution.

You will find a lot of information and illustrations about "finding and fitting" in this book. Connected with God, clear on your vision, confident in your unique role, you now are ready to move along the pathway to considering who you need to collaborate with you.

Collaboration

Who you need on your team and how to recruit, select, develop, and release them gets a lot of attention in the following pages. You will discover that not every idea will work in your circumstance but that some will. The up-front question at the moment becomes, then, where do I find them? Well, we have two answers to that question: You can pray hard and you can work smart.

Danielle worked in a large church in the city as the missions and outreach coordinator. Every day driving to work she passed by a large building surrounded by several smaller buildings sitting on a large piece of property landscaped as if it were a park.

Without noticeable signage the property appeared to be a city park.

Every day back and forth she drove, gradually becoming curious, even sensing God drawing her attention to this place. More time went by and she felt led to pray for this place and the people it represented as she passed by. Finally, she decided to pull in and drive around the parking lots to see if she could discover more about this place that the Lord would not release her from in her imagination. A small sign nearly overgrown by hedges told her it was a church and not a park. Okay, well, that made sense, sort of, and off she went, happy to continue praying for the place.

But the compulsion didn't stop. As weeks went by she found herself parking the car and walking around the property, praying for its ministry. At last she mustered the courage to walk into the office, announcing to the secretary, "You don't know who I am and I really don't know why I am here, but God told me this is the place I need to be."

Without blinking an eye the secretary said, "You need to talk to the pastor!"

When the pastor appeared and introductions were made he said simply, "Come in. I have been praying for you."

You see, this pastor had been asked to turn around a church in decline. With no staff except the part-time secretary and no resources, he couldn't scratch together the resources needed to find and hire the staff that was needed if the church were to grow. So, every day, he got on his knees praying that God would call just the right person to this place and walk them in the front door. Here she was, willing to volunteer without pay, with a doctorate in church planting and the call to serve on her heart.

Today that church is involved in ministry to the homeless, those in foster care, those in need of counseling, preschool for the impoverished, inner-city ministries in the Southwest, and missions in Nepal and Cambodia, and no one to credit for it but God.

That same church went on to build an all-star staff with only one of them showing up on the doorstep in similar fashion. The rest came by hard, smart work based upon solid human resources practices: create job descriptions, advertise, screen résumés, use telephone screening interviews, check credentials and references, have job candidates interview with staff and elders, test them if possible in the role, and hire them with a probationary period. Hiring with your head is hard work that needs prayer. In the end, by praying hard and working smart, you will assemble your dream team. Now all you need to do is enable and release the team members for ministry.

Commission

Enabling, sending, and releasing are important concepts we discuss in this book, and you will find a number of ideas and tools to support those activities. The foundation is laid in the ownership of the ministry you develop in your people. They need to believe they have appropriate freedom to act within their sphere of responsibility (what they "own"), while at the same time feeling some degree of responsibility for the entire ministry (what others "own"). They will need to understand the difference between management and leadership and which you are asking them to provide to the body. They will need to be able to differentiate between autocratic or hierarchical leadership and facilitative leadership and have mastered a number of different leadership styles and know when to use them.

This begins with your modeling these things, which assumes you are already at a place where you can do these things well enough to reproduce them in others. The idea behind this kind of commissioning is simple: "The things which you have heard from me in the presence of many witnesses, entrust these to faithful men who will be able to teach others also" (2 Timothy 2:2 NASB). Paul launched Timothy after careful preparation and not just with words of commissioning like, "Go get 'em, tiger!" or other motivational speeches. Those we commission will reproduce what we have modeled. Better to have been intentional about their preparation and therefore confident when we release them for ministry that they have been commissioned thoroughly. Once you and your team are up and running, you will need to remember to rest.

Comfort

Some days for both of us it feels like we are going at the speed of light with our hair on fire honking at our own taillights. That craziness moves from us to those we lead in ministry. At some point we all need to rest, and not just physically. We need soul maintenance that restores our emotions, strengthens our spirituality, and refreshes our connections with those we love, as well as God. None of us want to rust out. But on the other hand, we cannot afford to burn out, either. Part of our job as leaders is to care for our staff—to truly shepherd them—including modeling Sabbath moments for them and insisting upon their engagement in rest as well.

We need to make sure that in the midst of ministry we do not lose the rhythm of rest. Our very temperaments that drive our success invariably suppose that action and accomplishment are better than rest. If we go long enough without soul maintenance, we will lose our way. The absence of rest and reflection in our lives has more than just personal consequences. It influences the way we build and sustain our teams, determines how we respond to the trials and suffering of others, and shapes our ideas about healing and peace. Ultimately it hypnotizes us into believing we don't need rest, and the rhythm, the sweet music of God's refreshing, is lost.

George and Kristen argued often about vacations in their early years. She grew up in the city and her father worked downtown. Their rhythm of rest when it came to vacations was to take one or two weeks at a time around spring break from school, summer vacations, and over the Christmas holidays when employers and school districts anticipate and plan for these breaks. George grew up on a farm. You couldn't take long breaks with all that had to go on. He got used to taking lots of small breaks—just three or four days at a time—growing up. When George became a pastor, with all the pressures and commitments that go with that role, and they both agreed it was time for a break—well, you can see the impasse.

What they finally decided upon was doing both. Every three months they disappear for two to three days, and twice a year they take longer breaks of one to two weeks. Sometimes some of this is tacked onto a speaking engagement. Sometimes it takes advantage of the Sunday the elders want their pastor to take off between sermon series. Sometimes it is a stand-alone trip away from home and church, not related to anything else. The goal wasn't to fit church, conferences, kids and grandkids, and the need for rest into a busy schedule. The goal was to establish a rhythm of rest.

But it is more than just taking a break. Each day and each week must have those moments of rest that balance stretching experiences with nourishing ones. It could be a nap, undistracted time with the kids, a date with your sweetheart, an extended quiet time, a personal Bible study done for no other reason than your curiosity, walking the dog, a good book to read, an engaging movie to watch, or just sitting quietly for an hour.

If you do these things, your team will, too. They will be better for it, and you will have set them up to finish well.

Completion

Dave worked with me for years and had the reputation of being so single-minded at times that he could get himself into a jam in a heartbeat. He took a shortcut through the hospital kitchen once to meet me at the other end of a parallel corridor. Waiting, all I could hear was the rattle, clang, bang, and skittering of metal objects on a tile floor, very loud and very attention-getting. Here is what happened:

Moving quickly through the other door, Dave had to move aside as someone came out of the walk-in refrigerator with a case of hamburger meat in his arms. In his haste, Dave didn't see the stacks of paper cups on the rolling tray to his right, ready to be distributed elsewhere, and bumped into the cart, which began to tip over. Jumping back, he tripped the hamburger guy, who fell forward, launching the case of hamburger toward the dish rack waiting in front of the industrial dishwasher. The case of hamburger ended up on top as if it, too, were lined up for a rinse. That explained the first clatter and shatter of dishes.

Meanwhile, Dave had lurched forward off balance, trying not to run over the hamburger guy now on his knees on the floor. Taking several steps, each contributing more to his imbalance, Dave finally felt himself going down and reached out wildly high to his left and grabbed a pan hanging from the pot rack over the kitchen's island. His weight brought the pot rack down, sending pots and pans clattering all over the floor, explaining the metal-on-tile eruption heard by everyone in the corridor.

Getting to his feet and pulling his suit coat down, Dave stepped out the rear entrance and into the corridor where now a number of people had collected. Seemingly unperturbed, he looked around and affirmed, "I meant to do that." No sooner were the words out of his mouth than a frying pan clattered out the door, coming to rest by his heels; and the cart of paper cups, tipped at the beginning of his kamikaze trip through the kitchen, finally fell to the floor with its own contribution to the path of destruction laid down by my friend. Of course he did not intend to do any of that! None of us set out to consciously falter, fail, or fall.

If we are to help ensure that our projects, our people, and our ministries find completion in an upright manner and not in a disaster with the pieces rattling around our ankles, we need to keep our eyes on both the Savior and the goal. That takes leadership, planning, organization, and follow-up or evaluation. Be intentional about the pathway, and you will discover empowerment and extraordinary victory in all that you and your team pursue.

CHAPTER THREE

Motivation for Ministry

Without faith it is impossible to please God. —*Hebrews 11:6a NIV*

Being the boss was for me a way to control a life that for many years was out of control. As a kid, my life was submerged in constant chaos. An abusive, alcoholic father split up our family when my parents divorced and my brother and I were forced to live with Dad because Mom couldn't afford to support us. He drank a lot and worked a lot, so my brother and I pretty much raised each other.

Growing up in this uncertain and often dangerous world helped create in me a deep-seated need for control. With everything a mess all the time, I became a perfectionist, making sure everything in my control was organized and in order, including my emotions. What could be controlled became a safe haven. What could not be controlled was to be avoided. It took coming to Christ and entering the ministry to realize that a controlling perfectionist was not the ideal candidate for ministry leadership. What I desperately needed was a system overhaul from God. I think many people share this need for safety that works itself out as an annoying, controlling attitude. Some of the time leaders take charge more out of a need for control in their lives than from giftedness or calling.

These difficult underpinnings actually drive us to Christ, who redeems us and fills us with new purpose, using the very dysfunction we experience to create a place of contribution. Our

Common Leadership Wisdom: God calls me to *exercise leadership* in the ministry he has placed me in.

The Tilt: God calls me to *relinquish leadership to him* in the ministry he has placed me in.

leadership skills and experience, first practiced out of self-defense, become the very strengths Jesus calls us to use in serving others for the advancement of the kingdom (Romans 8:28). The challenge for us is to use these strengths for his purposes and no longer for our own.

Our inclination as leaders is to challenge everyone else to live up to the high standards we set for ourselves, but Jesus said a leader has to be the servant of everyone else (Mark 10:42-45). I was expecting perfection from myself and everyone else, too, but Jesus didn't. No one can ever live up to that expectation. Finally, a counselor helped me understand how the pain from my past had set me up for disappointment and failure. Even today, I have to be vigilant against the resurfacing of old issues. It's way too easy for them to distract me from being the husband, father, and ministry leader God designed me to be.

This vigilance extends to ministry as well. How much does my need for control play into my motivation for ministry? More than any other issue, how we deal with "control" in our lives can set us up for success—or set us up to sabotage all the good we earnestly desire to do. Empowering leaders means not only spending the time needed to develop them, but releasing them as well. They need freedom to develop their own style as ministry leaders, as well as freedom to fail. We need to fit them into a role in ministry based on their gifts and calling and not our expectations for how they ought to serve. These will all challenge a leader's natural bent for more, not less, control.

This assessment will help you identify how driven you may be as a leader and whether you can control your control issues:

Do You Have a Driven Personality?

True	False	
❑	❑	I am a competitive person.
❑	❑	I'm not very flexible.
❑	❑	I like to be in control of myself and my environment.
❑	❑	I often focus on details others find irrelevant.
❑	❑	I'm a perfectionist.
❑	❑	Some of my traits are at odds: I'm tidy in some areas of my life; messy in others. I'm conscientious about some things; negligent about others.
❑	❑	I give the appearance of confidence, but I feel insecure.
❑	❑	I set difficult goals and unrealistic expectations for myself, making myself vulnerable to feelings of guilt and failure.
❑	❑	I'm not comfortable "baring my soul." I like to keep my emotions to myself.
❑	❑	I don't relax easily.
❑	❑	I often act compulsively: I check and recheck the door to make sure it's locked. I return to the kitchen to satisfy myself that the stove is off.
❑	❑	I'm preoccupied with the future—always thinking about what's to come.
❑	❑	I'm dependable.
❑	❑	Being on time for appointments is a priority with me.
❑	❑	I like lists.
❑	❑	I worry too much.
❑	❑	I'm an extreme person: assertive sometimes; withdrawn at other times.
❑	❑	I expect total honesty and loyalty from the people closest to me.
❑	❑	I don't like spontaneity and surprises. I prefer to know what's going to happen so I can prepare well for it.

If you answered "true" to ten or more of these statements, you may have a tendency to be driven. Before you can truly realign your ministries and release your people into service as an empowering leader, you must surrender this matter of control to God. Now, if you have been involved in ministry of any kind for a while, this is not a new idea. But, here is the "tilt":

In theory, we all agree that Christ is the head of the church, but in practice our tendency is to keep taking control of our own lives and ministries. Maybe you've heard that the problem with living sacrifices is they keep crawling off the altar (Romans 12:1-2). It's true. We've *got* to relinquish the right of leadership to Christ. It's a daily, sometimes minute-by-minute decision, but it's critical to keep our alignment from slipping. Notice that it is the right to leadership that is the focus here and not your need for or exercise of control.

It is too easy to say that driven people have "control issues" because they have a high need to be self-directed or even self-protective. All of us need boundaries in our relationships, our work, and our social environment. Competition and the struggle to succeed also contribute to the energy or drive we put into what we do. These are all part of our daily lives; but life is not an experience that can be controlled, and therein lies the contradiction between healthy self-regulation and unrealistic efforts to rein in things beyond our power or ability to control.

Control issues begin to emerge when a child is eighteen months to three years of age as the child begins to experience relationships through feelings of being controlled. Childhood consists of lots of experiences in which we have to give up what we want and go along with someone else's will. When this includes threatening or neglectful situations, a pattern develops of exercising control in order to make things work out all right. As an adult, control allows us to repress our feelings, perform in ways we believe are acceptable to others, shield us from being weak and vulnerable, avoid feelings of powerlessness, and stay away from empathy, compassion, and anything else that we believe represents loss of control. "How much?" is the important question. How much of this control is normal and healthy and how much of this control represents dysfunction? Tough to say—a lot depends on the person, the situation, and the focus of efforts to control.

One measure is to ask yourself how much your sense of well-being revolves around the feeling of being in control and how much anxiety you experience when you are not in control. Control in life can be elusive. When we feel overwhelmed by our situation, we react and try harder to control the people and circumstances of our daily lives. Sometimes this trying harder is experienced by others as our having a driven personality.

As leaders we may feel the need to be in charge and manage the lives of others. By controlling certain aspects of our lives as well as others', we create an illusion of power and independence. Our leadership is exercised in these moments for our benefit alone rather than for the good of others in accomplishing our ministry goals. This makes it impossible to release ourselves or others for ministry and will not change until we relinquish leadership of the ministry to Jesus Christ. God has gifted and called us to serve his church, and for many of us that means exercising leadership. As we do that we need to be sure that we are leading for the right purpose—his glory and not our safety, security, or significance.

The element of control marks an important distinction between management and leadership, though we often use the terms interchangeably. When we talk about management, the focus is primarily on the management of things: schedules, resources, logistics, and such. Obviously, this involves people because people do the work. When we talk about leadership, the focus is primarily on people and the use of authority to influence or require others to act in concert with our directions or desires. Ministry is first about people and secondarily about things.

A tilt in perspective shows us that influencing change in people and groups for the advancement of the kingdom of God is the function of leadership, not management. Great managers do not necessarily make great leaders, and great leaders do not necessarily make great managers. If you are going to empower others, build hope into their lives, and release them for ministry, you must practice authentic leadership. Management by definition is all about control. Leadership is about movement and direction, about progressive release and not about control.

By acknowledging who we are in Christ in terms of our weaknesses as well as our strengths, we remove our temperament from the equation. God will use our temperament in all of its facets for his glory *if we let him*. For me, the crux of the matter is whether I have surrendered my right to lead, to be in charge, to make decisions, to direct the activities of others, and to control outcomes. Jesus Christ must lead through me, using all of who I am—the good, the bad, and the ugly. Am I allowing this to happen, or am I the one still in charge in the core of my being?

As difficult as it is to make that initial surrender to Christ, staying surrendered day after day after day is even harder. We know we have strengths and abilities, and it's easy to start relying on them. We're aware of the difficulties that arise in ministry; we're just not always sure we trust our volunteers to be up to the challenge. Rather than trusting Christ, or trusting Christ in others, we constantly wrestle with the temptation to take charge.

Leading from the Second Chair

To reach that place of full surrender, we must learn to lead from the second chair. In an orchestra, the second-chair violinist not only has to master the music but also has to follow the lead of the first-chair musician. This is why most conductors will tell you the hardest instrument to play is second fiddle, and why they look for musicians that have *surrendered* their right to the first chair.

Second chair is where *all* of us must lead from if we are genuinely submitted to Christ. An empowering leader understands that even the senior pastor leads from the second chair—because the first chair must be occupied by Christ himself. Psalm 86:11 says, "Teach me, LORD, what you want me to do, and I will obey you faithfully; teach me to serve you with complete devotion" (GNT). If Christ is not conducting the orchestra of your life and ministry, it's not just that you won't succeed—you *can't* succeed.

One thing that has helped me lead from the second chair is monitoring my devotion to God. I meditate on the words of the psalmist quoted above, especially the part about "what you want me to do." And I focus on Paul's admonition to "work hard and do not be lazy. Serve the Lord with a heart full of devotion" (Romans 12:11 GNT).

The question I constantly ask myself is, "What is distracting me from being fully devoted to God?" In reality each of us is distracted from God's service in some way, every day. This distraction seems to be a natural result of living in a fallen world. But if we are honest with ourselves and willing to listen when others catch us playing as if we were seated in the first chair, we'll gradually improve our ability to consistently lead from the second chair.

"I want to let go, but I'm scared." These honest words from a man I met after a conference session reminded me that surrender is difficult—no matter how long we've been following and serving Christ. As we'd closed the session, I had challenged the room to take their first step toward empowering leadership—through surrendering it all to God. The man who came to speak with me after the session was a senior pastor.

"Do you have plans for lunch?" I asked him. For the next hour, we sat and talked about life and our ministries. From the outside, this pastor had it all: a large church, a big staff, and a nice paycheck. But inside he was in knots.

As he shared some of his emotional and relational struggles with me, one thing became crystal clear. This pastor needed to control the people and circumstances that filled his world. I shook my head in amazement as I once again observed God's ability to connect people, for I could honestly say it takes one to know one. His life had become gripped by what I call "devotional distractions"—issues that break our connection with God. What he desperately needed was to experience the freedom that comes from letting go of the need to be in charge, and letting God lead his life and ministry.

"Where is God in your life?" I asked. It was the same question a mentor had asked me many years before.

"Not in the first chair," he admitted.

So I read him Psalm 139 and asked him to search his own heart and life for what he was holding on to. "Identify those things," I told him, "and then give them to God.

"Just talk to God. You don't have to be formal. Share your raw feelings. God already knows them. He simply wants to hear from one of his prized trophies."

Right then and there, he opened up before God, and his emotions ran the gambit from anger to sadness to joy. Tears streamed down his face.

"Are you okay?" I asked when the flood began.

"These are tears of joy," he smiled. And the man before me was not the same one I'd been talking to moments before. It was as if he'd had an "extreme makeover" right in front of me. God had clearly taken his burdens and replaced them with his love, grace, and mercy.

This kind of renovation is available for everyone—including you. Learning to see God in that first chair and follow his lead is critical for us as pastors and ministry leaders. Jesus tells us in John 15:5 that apart from him we can do nothing. That truth is not new to you, but this one might be: We live in such an instant society we forget that transformation takes time. We must get connected to God, and we must be ever mindful of maintaining that connection.

36

Devotional Distractions

It is easy to become distracted from that connection. The list of potential "devotional distractions" is long, and it varies for each person. As I look back through my own journal, I find ten issues that have disconnected me from my heavenly Father, issues that can still break that connection when I let my guard down:

1. Pain from my past
2. Prideful spirit
3. Perfectionist attitude
4. Pleasing everyone
5. Procrastination
6. Peer pressure
7. Past failures
8. People in my life or past
9. Personal messages
10. Poor lifestyle—rest, diet, exercise

Each of us has our own set of devotional distractions. They continually sidetrack us from God's plan by disconnecting us from the Lord and tricking us into following our own inclinations. Thinking like God thinks isn't easy. God himself tells us, "My thoughts are nothing like your thoughts, . . . and my ways are far beyond anything you could imagine" (Isaiah 55:8 NLT). Yet he promises that our lives will be transformed into living demonstrations of God's "good and acceptable and perfect will" when we allow him to renew our minds (Romans 12:2 NKJV).

What future could your devotional distractions keep you from embracing? God wants you to identify them and then hand them over to his control.

If you watch runners train for competition, you occasionally will see some wearing weights around their ankles. The additional weight strengthens their legs and increases stamina. When it comes to race time, however, you will never see them settling into the starting blocks with those weights still strapped to their ankles. When it's time to run the race, you don't want anything weighing you down. Without the added "stuff," the runners are free to fly.

A lot of ministry leaders run their races with "stuff" weighing them down. This kind of additional baggage keeps us from being as useful to the Lord as we could be. We get tangled up in these sins and fail to run our best race. The writer of the letter to the Hebrews urged his audience to "strip off every weight that slows us down, especially the sin that so easily trips us up. And let us run with endurance the race God has set before us" (12:1 NLT).

So, once we have eliminated the devotional distractions—those things that keep us from connecting with God and therefore prevent us from maintaining an attitude of surrender—we need to shed the weighty stuff we don't need to be carrying around. Rick Warren likes to describe these weighty things using an alliteration that has influenced my thinking over the years. Typically, these include worries, wounds, wrongs, weaknesses, and wishes.

Worries. All of us, to one degree or another, feel worry, or as we call it today, "stress." For some of us, it's merely an occasional feeling prompted by unusual circumstances. For many others, however, worry is a chronic problem. We spend endless hours fretting over things we want to change—things we know are beyond our control. Over time, the burden begins to weigh us down.

The Bible tells us: "Cast your cares on the LORD and he will sustain you; he will never let the righteous fall" (Psalm 55:22 NIV). The word *cast* means we are to literally *heave* our burdens at God. All the stress that weighs us down is nothing to God. Billy Graham once said that anxiety is the natural result when our hopes are centered in anything short of God and his will for us. Our hopes and plans for our lives are the very things that, when taken out of perspective, lead to anxious thoughts and emotions.

Many people I know—myself included—worry about work, relationships, finances, health issues, and not seeing their dreams come to fruition. We worry about not being accepted or about the difficulty of overcoming sinful habits. Others struggle because they don't feel forgiven by God, or are worried that they can't live up to a purpose or mission they have agreed to.

The servant of God who wants to be completely aligned with God's purpose for his or her ministry must unload these burdens. What worries are weighing you down and keeping you from running your race with endurance? Go find some small stones and write each worry on a separate rock. Now, go find a nearby ravine, pond, or even a Dumpster and heave all your worries away. God knows what to do with them.

Wounds. Many of us also are wounded in spirit. Perhaps someone we trusted betrayed us or a gossip spread lies about us. Perhaps we simply failed to reach some hoped-for goal and we suffer from a self-inflicted injury. While physical wounds usually heal, emotional wounds can remain open for many years—often reopened again and again. Even if you think the wound in your soul is beyond repair, the Bible promises that God "heals the brokenhearted and binds up their wounds" (Psalm 147:3 NIV). God is waiting for each of us to give him our greatest pains and deepest scars. The Great Physician promises he will heal our wounds. Freedom and healing are found only when we release them to God.

Wrongs. Very few things hinder our alignment with God more than feelings of guilt. All of us have done things in the past— sometimes in the very recent past—to hurt others and embarrass ourselves. We can wrong others with our words and our actions. Giving our wrongs to God starts with confession—admitting them to God and to those we've hurt so we can receive forgiveness. The Bible tells us that confession arising from a sincerely repentant heart opens the way for us to receive forgiveness and cleansing from God: "If we confess our sins, he is faithful and just and will forgive us our sins and purify us from all unrighteousness" (1 John 1:9 NIV).

39

Admitting our wrongs doesn't come easily to us. Our pride stands in the way. But when Christ sets us free from guilt, we are "free indeed" (John 8:36 NIV). We discover the marvelous joy that comes from realizing that there is no condemnation in Christ (Romans 8:1). And we find strength and confidence when we recognize that continued feelings of guilt over sins God has forgiven are nothing more than a ploy of Satan to keep us from experiencing the abundant life Christ purchased for us on the cross.

Weaknesses. Our society encourages us to play up our strengths and hide our weaknesses. But do you realize that your weaknesses are part of God's design for your life? He actually gave you the shortcomings you have on purpose—to give him an opportunity to show his strength in your life. In fact, the Apostle Paul said he bragged about his weaknesses: "To keep me from becoming proud, I was given a thorn in my flesh, a messenger from Satan to torment me and keep me from becoming proud. Three different times I begged the Lord to take it away. Each time he said, 'My grace is all you need. My power works best in weakness.' So now I am glad to boast about my weaknesses, so that the power of Christ can work through me" (2 Corinthians 12:7-9 NLT).

Do you think God can't use your weakness? The Lord promises he will use it to bless others and glorify his name if you will give it to him. I have seen him do it in my own life and in the lives of literally hundreds of others. He can do this in your life, too. In fact, he longs to. Where do you need to see God's strength in your ministry? Give him your weakness.

Wishes. Our desires and dreams can present either obstacles to God's work through us or pathways that guide us toward turning his dreams for us into reality. The difference springs from whether those desires and dreams are my wishes for myself or come from his plan to advance his kingdom through me. The Bible says, "Seek first his kingdom and his righteousness, and all these things will be given to you as well"

(Matthew 6:33 NIV). What wishes, dreams, and desires do you need to surrender today?

Surrender

Motivation is another way of describing where we focus our energy, what we give ourselves to with passion, how we address needs we see in our own lives and the lives of others. No one can motivate us. Motivation comes from within when we are moved to meet those perceived needs. Our motivation in ministry, therefore, reflects what needs we are trying to meet. If we are working hard at controlling our world and the outcomes of our ministry and not working hard at shedding what encumbers us and maintaining that vital personal connection with Jesus, we are not living surrendered lives. We may even be unconsciously expecting the ministry to meet our needs for safety, security, and significance. It is to Christ that we look for these things and not to the ministry itself.

Surrender does not mean we spinelessly shrink into our corner and let others lead. God has called us, gifted us, equipped us, and sent us into the ministry to make a difference, to assertively and even aggressively use those skills and talents at his direction. This is not the calling of the faint of heart, but a calling that demands initiative, action, and ultimately courageous victory! The Apostle Paul pictures this partnership in ministry using two very strong words: *walk* by the Spirit and be *led* by the Spirit (Galatians 5:16-18). "Walk" and "be led" are both imperatives, giving us a picture of both parties assertively fulfilling their roles in the partnership. God leads, we follow; both are acts of the will requiring volitional cooperation—first chair, second chair—both doing their parts.

If my motivation in ministry is to be obedient to the call of God on my life, fulfilling that call in the context of his design and purpose for me, then my human foibles, my personality, my weaknesses don't matter at all. If, however, my motivation is to somehow live and minister self-righteously, self-protectively, or self-directedly—then I will endure the frustration of living in my will and not in his perfect will for me. If we are to build hope in a new generation of spiritual leaders, if we are to develop and empower leaders for the kingdom of God, then we must look only to Christ in serving the ministry and not require that the ministry serve us. Every day we must check our motivation and surrender anew to the lordship of Jesus Christ.

CHAPTER FOUR

Igniting Your Vision

God . . . is able, through his mighty power at work within us, to accomplish infinitely more than we might ask or think.
—Ephesians 3:20 NLT

When Martin Luther King, Jr., took his stand on the steps of the Lincoln Memorial on August 28, 1963, there wasn't much in American history to justify his faith that the United States would become a place where the sons of former slaves and the sons of former slave owners would sit down together at the table of brotherhood. But barely four months after writing his famous *Letter from Birmingham Jail*, King stood before a crowd of 250,000 people in Washington, D.C., and delivered a powerful speech that inspired much of the nation with a vision of basic equality for all Americans, regardless of the color of their skin.

Giving a fine speech was hardly the end of the matter, however. During the ten months before President Lyndon Johnson signed the Civil Rights Act of 1964, peaceful civil rights protests continued to be met with violent resistance, and King paid with his own life less than four years later. While much of his dream still remains to be realized, King's faith and courage helped change an entire nation by transforming individual hearts that in turn transformed neighborhoods, then cities, and then entire states.

God has placed in your heart already a vision for you and your ministry that may seem impossible but, if released, can be just as world-changing as Dr. King's dream. John 14:12 says, "I can guarantee this truth: Those who believe in me will do the things that I am doing. They will do even greater things because I am going to the Father" (GWT). What an awesome promise! We can do greater things!

The framework for creating our vision for ministry has already been laid out for us in Acts 2:42: "They were continually devoting themselves to the apostles' teaching and to fellowship, to the breaking of bread and to prayer" (NASB). Teaching the word of God, continuing to support one another, expressing gratitude for all that Christ has accomplished, and continuing in prayer—all while meeting together—is the model we find coming out of those early days of ministry after Jesus ascended into heaven. This is described in more detail by the various apostles later in the New Testament:

He gave some as apostles, and some as prophets, and some as evangelists, and some as pastors and teachers, for the equipping of the saints for the work of service, to the building up of the body of Christ. (Ephesians 4:11-12 NASB)

Let us consider how to stimulate one another to love and good deeds, not forsaking our own assembling together, as is the habit of some, but encouraging one another; and all the more as you see the day drawing near. (Hebrews 10:24-25 NASB)

Above all, keep fervent in your love for one another, because love covers a multitude of sins. Be hospitable to one another without complaint. As each one has received a special gift, employ it in serving one another as good stewards of the manifold grace of God. (1 Peter 4:8-10 NASB)

"A new commandment I give to you, that you love one another, even as I have loved you, that you also love one another. By this all men will know that you are My disciples, if you have love for one another." (John 13:34-35 NASB)

Jesus came up and spoke to them, saying, "All authority has been given to Me in heaven and on earth. Go therefore and make disciples of all the nations, baptizing them in the name of the Father and the Son and the Holy Spirit, teaching them to observe all that I commanded you; and lo, I am with you always, even to the end of the age." (Matthew 28:18-20 NASB)

With the fundamental mission identified for us already, it just remains to be determined what God has uniquely designed us for and called us to within that mission. What excites us, fills us with anticipation, and gives us great joy in the doing? In other words, what is the vision that drives us and our ministry? When we are serving according to the purpose God has given us, our work seems almost effortless—even tackling the hard things. But when we operate outside our design and calling or from a lack of purpose and vision, everything takes effort. We end the day in frustration and fatigue rather than with a sense of joy that anticipates tomorrow. When you are doing the work that God approves, life is an adventure!

One Clear Vision

Some of us may serve in ministries that either have reached a plateau or are in decline, leaving leaders feeling disheartened. Discouragement is contagious—if left uncurbed, it spreads to the entire ministry.

One reason for this is that we are confused about vision. If someone in your ministry asked what your vision is, or what the ministry's identity is—how would you answer? Could you answer? Empowering leaders have a clearly articulated personal vision and can describe for anyone who asks what the ministry is all about. If we are going to see God's dream for our ministries come true, we have to create a clear

Common Leadership Wisdom: Involving stakeholders *in creating a strategic plan* can ignite the vision.

The Tilt: Involving stakeholders *in pursuit of the vision*, regularly reviewing and updating the strategic plan, will keep the fires burning bright.

vision that everybody shares. Nothing revitalizes a discouraged ministry faster than rediscovering its purpose. Your first responsibility as a leader is to recapture a clear vision of what God wants to do in and through your ministry, igniting a vision that will reproduce itself in the hearts and minds of everyone involved.

Cornerstone Church, a medium-sized, purpose-driven church, was stagnating; meeting regularly for no clear purpose, shrinking instead of growing, with no clear picture of how to move forward. A new senior pastor was called, one with experience creating vision and leading teams. In the first few months it became clear that the ministry needed some key things. From a practical perspective this included offering multiple worship services, adding additional staff, and improving the quality of ministry. More fundamentally, they needed to develop a distinct identity and create a long-range, culturally relevant and biblically appropriate strategic plan.

These last two needs struck at the heart of purpose, mission, and vision. The senior pastor led the ministry team through a strategic planning process that evaluated the basic functions of ministry from a biblical perspective, assessed the needs of the community they were serving, and determined who they were going to be based upon where God was already leading and working. If the leader doesn't have a vision, the ministry won't have a vision. If the ministry doesn't have a vision, the people will scatter to other ministries that do have a compelling vision (Proverbs 29:18).

Here is what the pastor was passionate about—influencing change as invisibly as possible in people and groups for the advancement of the kingdom of God. After working through a process of understanding their identity and capturing this in a statement of mission, the team boiled their vision down to "Kingdom Minded, Family Centered, Community Focused." Within a year the ministry had doubled in size as people found excitement and energy in a single, clear vision. A leader with a clear vision is a passionate, energetic, inspiring leader able to inspire and empower others.

Creating a vision, understanding your mission, and crafting a strategic ministry plan are not new concepts in ministry. Actually using, reviewing, and updating these concepts on a regular basis, however, is a new experience for many ministries.

One clear vision is crucial, and it is obvious that planning is also crucial for ensuring that vision comes to life. But what happens to most strategic plans is that after year one into executing the plan, it gets set aside, forgotten. After all, it seems like we are all off to a good start with our direction set! What about all those assumptions made in planning? What about contingencies you relied on? What about all the things that have changed in the ministry since that first year? Revisiting and updating the strategic plan are actually more important than creating the plan in the first place. Vision doesn't become crystal clear for most people until they have lived with it, worked with it, and put it into practice for two to three years. Ideally, get your team together to course-correct every six months and review the entire plan once each year. That will help you stay on track with one clear vision.

Don't Settle for Less

As you refocus on God's vision for your ministry, it is absolutely critical that you not settle for anything less than a divine ministry dream. Isaiah 55:8-9 tells us that God's thoughts are as far above our own as the heavens are above the earth. When Jesus clearly explained his vision of death and resurrection to his disciples, Peter rejected it. Do you remember what Jesus said to him? "Get out of my way, Satan! You aren't thinking the way God thinks but the way humans think" (Mark 8:33 GWT).

Settling for anything less than God's vision actually puts you in opposition to God. When refocusing on God's dream for your ministry, you've got to seek God's thoughts. Be sure to consider these seven values in making sure your vision aligns with God's dream for you and your ministry. As you craft your dream with God, ask yourself these questions:

1. Does the dream align with the Bible?
2. Will the dream show God's love in practical ways?
3. Will the dream take extraordinary faith?
4. Will the dream use ordinary people to fulfill it?
5. Will the dream lead people toward living servant lives?
6. Will the dream embrace the giftedness within the body?
7. Will the dream make God the hero and me his helper?

At Saddleback Church, we dream of a day when "every member is ministering through their God-given S.H.A.P.E. (spiritual gifts, heart, abilities, personality, experiences) so that all of the needs within the Body are met by the Body." That vision statement is founded on 1 Peter 4:10: "Each one should use whatever gift he has received to serve others, faithfully administering God's grace in its various forms" (NIV).

Our dream reflects the seven vision values: It aligns with the Bible. It emphasizes showing God's love in practical ways. It does and will continue to take extraordinary faith to fulfill. It is all about empowering ordinary people to do extraordinary work through servant hearts. It requires us to be servants, not masters. It fully embraces each person discovering and living out his or her God-given individual giftedness. The result is that God is glorified.

This proved to be equally true for Cornerstone Church. Whether it is a large or small ministry makes no difference. God has something on his heart for each ministry that we need to identify and tap into, fitting together the pieces he has already assembled for us to use around that singular clear vision. In working with different churches and denominational structures, or mission organizations and Christian nonprofit ministries, and even in the world of Christian-based companies, we have found this to be true over and over again. Without a clear vision that has passion behind it, nothing gets empowered, especially people.

After the congregation at Family Community Church in San Jose, California, moved into a larger building, the adult ministries pastor had a vision to make sure church members did not lose sight of their mission statement: *People growing in relationship with Christ, church, and community.* This overarching purpose definitely aligns with the Bible, shows God's love in practical ways, and uses ordinary people to fulfill it. But did it require extraordinary faith? Well, if you've worked toward accomplishing a big goal for God, you know that any huge effort requires faith in God and faith in people to get the job done. For this ministry leader, it took the form of a network team to help direct those ordinary people into ministries that allowed them to use their gifts in serving the body of Christ. As a result, the ministry has an active congregation, working together to make God the hero to their neighbors and to the world. It begins with you and a clear vision.

An Audacious Dream

Every great breakthrough for God's kingdom starts with a dream in someone's heart. Recognizing our natural tendency to draw attention to ourselves or to be admired for our success, some ministry leaders are reluctant to let their imaginations run wild when it comes to clarifying a vision for the church. We encourage you to simply ask, "Who will be glorified by this dream?" If the answer is you, then it is definitely the wrong dream. But if the dream brings glory to God and magnifies him, go for it! So many people think it's prideful to have an ambitious dream. Who do you think placed those desires in your heart? Psalm 37:4 says, "Delight yourself in the LORD; and He will give you the desires of your heart" (NASB).

What about you? What are the desires of your heart for your ministry? Draw a portrait of where God wants to take this ministry. Clarifying a specific, challenging vision attracts commitment. People *want* to give their lives to something bigger than themselves, something that gives them meaning and significance. They *want* to be a part of something worthwhile. Jesus challenged his followers to total commitment: "Any of you who does not give up everything he has cannot be my disciple" (Luke 14:33 NIV). Can you picture what it would look like for you to be part of a ministry that fully releases the gifts and passions of the people for God's glory? Here are some practical steps you can take to help you get started with dreaming big:

1. Get with God—The first question you should ask yourself is, "Do my desires make God the hero?" We want to make God the hero in everything we do. If our desires don't do that, they may be selfish ambitions. When we find our delight in God, then his desires become the desires of our heart and he is free to make those dreams come true.

2. Face your fears—What frightens you more: the fear of failure or the fear of success? It may sound crazy, but it is true that people are more often done in by the fear of success than by the possibility they might fail. Ask God to show you what is keeping you from expecting and attempting great things, and don't be afraid of what other people might say. Solomon wrote, "Fearing people is a dangerous trap, but trusting the LORD means safety" (Proverbs 29:25). We know from Paul that God does not give us a spirit of fear (2 Timothy 1:7). God wants us to admit our fears and then step out in the confidence that comes from knowing who he is and who he has made us to be.

3. Manage your motives—You also need to ask yourself, "What motivates this dream?" Sometimes motives aren't entirely God-honoring. Colossians 3:23-24 tells us, "Whatever you do, work at it with all your heart, as working for the Lord, not for men, since you know that you will receive an inheritance from the Lord as a reward" (NIV). Take a hard look in the mirror and identify your motives. Remember, motives are another way of describing the energy we put behind meeting perceived needs.

4. Ask for assistance—Give people permission to ask you what your dreams are and why. Do you have an accountability partner? You can ask each other the tough questions you both know need to be confronted. "The heart is hopelessly dark and deceitful, a puzzle that no one can figure out" (Jeremiah 17:9 *The Message*). Balancing that truth, we also know that "the more good advice you get, the more likely you are to win" (Proverbs 24:6b GNT).

5. Count the cost—God-sized dreams are costly. It may be a financial cost that requires you and others to make sacrifices. It may be a relational cost, like the price your family pays when you travel, or the rejection or ridicule you will experience from others. Luke 14:28 says, "Suppose you want to build a tower. You would first sit down and figure out what it costs. Then you would see if you have enough money to finish it" (GWT). You need to decide if your dream carries a price tag that you may not be willing or able to pay right now. It may be that the time is not yet right for your dream to come true.

6. Give it a go—Conventional wisdom says you plot out your dream in detail before you start trying to make it happen. The truth, however, is that it's only after you start moving toward your goal that you discover the exact shape of the dream. Each of the successful ministries we have described here fail more often than they succeed, but that's how they stay aligned with where God is leading. Hold on to the promise of Proverbs 16:3: "Commit to the LORD whatever you do, and your plans will succeed" (NIV).

Time to Dream

Now that we have had a chance to think about a clear vision that can ignite excitement and capture the imagination, and you have realistically looked at some of the things in ministry that must fit well together for this vision to have a chance to succeed, it is time to dream. It may be true at this point that you need to give more attention to working these things out, that you really don't have enough of the pieces of the puzzle on the table yet to constructively dream. In truth, vision casting and dreaming are iterative processes. That is, you go back and forth between the two as the Holy Spirit guides the process into riveting clarity.

So, take a shot at dreaming right now and then go back and forth between your vision and your dream. Bathe it in prayer. Sleep on it. Talk to others about it. Use the tips we have laid out thus far to tilt your perspective and imagine God's desired future.

> Paint a word picture that describes in a few short sentences what the ministry will look like in ten years. Be creative in your description and not simply factual. This is your dream!

Does your description match what God wants for your ministry? What do you see that needs to change in your dream? Once you have come to a place where God has ignited your soul around this dream, it is time to move on to considering obstacles to overcome.

Every dream has a dream-buster, every vision a death waiting! This, too, is part of the process. The writer of the letter to the Hebrews reminds us that the maturity of an idea is developed through hard work over time by those "who because of practice have their senses trained to discern good and evil" (5:14 NASB). Overcoming obstacles, rekindling a vision that may have died, teaches us in practical ways how to guard our vision and direct our passion.

CHAPTER FIVE

Guarding Your Vision

We entered the land you sent us to explore, and it is indeed a bountiful country—a land flowing with milk and honey. . . . But the people living there are powerful, and their towns are large and fortified. We even saw giants there! —Numbers 13:27-28 NLT

Your dream for your ministry is going to face opposition. Just as it is the nature of things to change, it is in our nature to resist change. Already we have been asked to be honest with ourselves and willing to look at things differently—resolving control issues and releasing any anchors from our past in order to create a clear vision that can stand up to hard questions. This alone can be personally challenging. However, there are other giants in life and ministry to face that can encourage us to drag our feet, to be overly cautious, and to resist the changes we are already committed to make.

Launching into a new vision is a lot like learning to fly. Student pilots face many personal challenges they must overcome in order first even to qualify to fly a plane with the help of an instructor. Mastery of certain knowledge, testing of basic skills, developing a minimum of experience, and facing a number of fears, the least of which is fear of failure, all create an internal struggle for the would-be pilot.

Then there is the solo flight: all alone for the very first time with no one to help if you get in trouble. The challenges are no longer just an internal struggle. You will find some intimidating obstacles to overcome externally as well. Then comes instrument

Common Leadership Wisdom: Every vision encounters unforeseen obstacles along the way.

The Tilt: Every vision *carries with it the solutions* it needs for obstacles along the way.

training and the difficulty in learning to trust something outside yourself, especially when all your senses are telling you that you are upside down! Learning to fly blind is not fun at all! No matter what your vision, in addition to feeling like you are alone, upside down, and have only God to trust, there are giants in the land that must be overcome. In helping ministries become empowered we have observed that guarding your vision often means dealing with three common giants that can keep your dream from getting off the ground and gaining altitude. These giants include the values, administration, and infrastructure that already exist in the ministry you seek to transform.

Now, most of us have previous experience with these issues as part of the process of implementing a vision. Here is the tilt: Rather than wait to discover these things experientially along the way, why not assess them in advance and make plans for the adaptations that will be necessary for your vision to succeed? If you are going to take your ministry to the next level, you will need to address these giants within your ministry first. What is that old axiom . . . an ounce of prevention is worth a pound of cure?

Values

Some ministries state that they value discipleship; some value evangelism. Others value fellowship or worship or ministry. It is easy to confuse the purposes of worship, fellowship, discipleship, ministry, and evangelism with the values that undergird these or any aspect of ministry. These are really just labels for specific outcomes in a purpose-driven ministry.

A set of driving values consists of six to eight values that are responsible for 90 percent of the organizational behaviors in the ministry. A value in this sense is a sustained belief held by key stakeholders that some behaviors or goals are preferable over others. Regardless of what you want to be as a ministry, this set determines what the ministry really is and how those you serve will experience the ministry. For example, an emphasis on certain value-driven behaviors (like connection with God or excellence in music) will lead to worship as an identifiable function in your ministry.

What is it that provides incentives for those behaviors in the first place? How do you know which values will produce the behaviors that result in a successful purpose-driven ministry? Let's say hypothetically that you are about to launch an outreach ministry and you want to build a team with the best chance of success. Driving values like influence, affiliation, public contact, helping society, and healthy pressure will help ensure a fruitful ministry. If your team doesn't possess those values, what can you do about it? More important, when you look at the team as a whole and the consensus of their driving values, are there any values that work against your success? Better to have these questions answered before you face the giant.

People not only have to be energized by your vision, they must have the right set of driving values to carry it out with passion and excitement. That is, they need to have in common an enduring conviction that certain modes of conduct or conditions are preferable in order to *naturally* produce the results that fulfilling the vision requires. Otherwise, when the reward for change (or enforcement of change) is removed, the ministry will regress to what *naturally* drove the group all along. Selecting on the basis of value-driven behaviors is key to staff retention and high volunteerism.

Administration

Administration refers to the impact of the leadership culture in the ministry and how this limits or releases volunteers and staff in crucial areas. Culture is another way of describing how people respond to the environment in which they find themselves. Habitual or patterned responses give rise to unwritten rules of the road, the accepted ways of doing things. This is no different in ministry and often is the source of land mines and other hidden obstacles of gigantic proportion. Usually conflict arises around four types of obstacles related to how the ministry is administrated:

Limited leadership—Many ministries call a new senior leader, only to have other leaders in the ministry handcuff the leader shortly after his or her arrival. The conflicts really heat up when the newcomer tries to exercise the authority that would help the ministry become everything God intends it to be. Determining who the functional leaders really are (*functional* meaning they may exercise influence without holding a position) in advance of implementing a new vision is important. What are their driving values? How can they be brought on board? Do they view you as an extension of their agenda, or themselves as serving the body under your leadership?

Marginal modeling—Some senior leaders talk about the importance of every member being a minister on mission, but they don't model it themselves. That undermines that value throughout the ministry and leads to staff and volunteer frustration. If you want to reproduce the right values in others, you must first model them. Folks will emulate what you demonstrate far more than what you preach; and if they happen to be the same thing, it is a powerful message indeed! My first day on the job as a new senior pastor started with plunging toilets. There was a need, no one was stepping up, and even before introductions were over I quietly stepped aside to put the women's restroom back in working order. Some thought, not having been introduced to me yet, that they had a new plumber! Later on, the lesson continued with Dumpster diving after erroneously discarded material. After a number of weeks the often-repeated lesson sank in—the new pastor values serving and no chore is too menial. It was a good team and they all stepped up to the standard, adopting as their own the value of service.

Job mismatch—This occurs when persons' strengths and passions aren't aligned with their roles and responsibilities. If there is a mismatch, the persons will over time become frustrated and see no value in empowering themselves or others. However, when all persons are operating within their God-given design, they will quickly see the need of inviting and investing in others. Each of us has a purpose and calling that has vocational implications for what we are best suited for in work and ministry. Intentional decisions about placement can remove a tremendous amount of unnecessary friction. If you could identify these hot points before you roll out your vision, what an incredible difference it could make!

Stagnant staff—People simply don't follow up in a timely, caring manner. Calls don't get returned, e-mails are left unread, and volunteers trying to find a place to serve get the feeling there is no place in ministry for them. If there is an overarching value that cuts across all sectors of the organization, it has got to be the worth of the individual. People who are marginalized by the system, no matter how well intended the staff, are still marginalized. What is the public perception of the ministry? Will this affect negatively any changes you want to make such that this needs to be worked on first before introducing anything new? Staff seldom perceive themselves in this negative manner and almost always assume they can be trusted to do the right thing every time. It is the blind spots that catch them up in failures only others perceive. That is why it is important to trust but verify. Trust your staff to do the right thing and periodically verify from the perspective of those they serve that the right things are really happening.

Infrastructure

Another giant that can prevent ministries from moving into empowerment is the lack of sustained structural support. This can be financial support, communications support, or leadership support, but most often is simply the lack of a strategic ministry plan that charts the course over the next few years. Without a plan, you are planning to fail, and no amount of financial support, communicating with the ministry and its constituents, or leadership will overcome a lack of intelligent planning. With each goal you have set, you should have already thought through the set of driving values necessary for its completion. With every objective you have identified, there should also be recognized practices that will lead to the fulfillment of the objective. With every action step required by the plan, you should already know what collective behaviors will be required to complete the task. Matching values, practices, and behaviors to the goals, objectives, and tasks is a function of cultural planning, a process often left out of strategic planning and a significant reason why many excellent plans with all the needed resources never are accomplished. We will look at these planning functions more in chapter 11.

These "giants" prevent many churches and ministries from entering the land of empowering ministry. Often leaders shrink from the challenge of thorough preparation before launching and thus fail to guard carefully the vision from what potentially lies ahead. But God's plan is for you and your ministry to experience the absolute best he has in store for you, and his desire is for you to follow him in faith as he overcomes the obstacles in your path. Remember, nothing is impossible with God!

When God was about to send his people into the promised land, he gave Moses a vision. He told Moses to send a team of men to explore the land of Canaan that he was giving them. When they got there, they saw that the land literally flowed with milk and honey—but it was inhabited by strong people, large people the Israelites thought they could not possibly overcome. There were giants in the land, and because of them, God's chosen people were ready to give up. But where would we be today if they had simply thrown in the towel and given in to their fears and weaknesses?

If you are discouraged by the giants in the land of your dreams, it is time to tilt: Trust God, do your homework, and march on in. No dream worth pursuing will be free from such obstacles, but it is the obstacles that often help us grow stronger. Even the children of Israel didn't get it right the first time, but that does not mean you have to wander in the wilderness before trying again.

Resistance to change is natural and often healthy. When that resistance is rooted in these organizational giants, there is a lot you can do about it before you become entangled in anything that threatens your dream. Be diligent in guarding your vision. It will be stretched and tested, all for good purpose. A belief does not become a conviction until it has been tested, and a conviction does not become a vision until it has been tried.

CHAPTER SIX

Finding Your Strengths and Style as a Leader

Like an open book, you watched me grow from conception to birth;
all the stages of my life were spread out before you,
the days of my life all prepared before I'd even lived one day.
—*Psalm 139:13-16* The Message

Eating grasshoppers was not my idea of a gourmet meal. Neither was the rabbit we'd had two days prior. But then, escape and evasion training wasn't about comfort in the first place. Living off the land, traveling long distances by night, navigating by the stars, climbing mountains, swimming rivers—it was all part of our endurance training. If any of us were shot down, the Marine Corps wanted us to get back safely.

The training wasn't just oriented toward the skills we might need. It was also designed to help us struggle well. Any great task is a struggle, and without endurance no one struggles well enough to succeed. So we learned to struggle well, repeating the lessons and practicing our skills until they were nearly second nature. Our instructors understood that the best preparation they could provide was not in the techniques or the skills but in the mental perspective that enables the kind of endurance that comes only from struggling well enough to be someone others can count on to overcome any obstacles.

The Apostle Paul also understood this idea of struggling well. One of the clearest statements Paul makes in this regard is found in Romans 12:1-2: "I urge you, brethren, by the mercies of God, to present your bodies a living and holy sacrifice, acceptable to God, which is your spiritual service of worship. And do not be conformed to this world, but be transformed by the renewing of your mind, so that you may prove what the will of God is, that which is good and acceptable and perfect" (NASB). When Paul used the phrases "present your bodies" and "do not be conformed" and "be transformed," he used grammar that illustrates for us a process drawn out over time rather than an event or a series of events.

In fact, the contrast between being "transformed" and being "conformed" is most strongly expressed in the original language of the New Testament. Though all of us experience constant pressure to cave in to how the world says we ought to live, Paul encourages us to refuse to give up and allow the world to take us captive. His version of escape and evasion training uses a different word—*transformation*—to describe struggling well. Paul says that we should be transformed, *metamorphousthe*, using the same word from which we get our word for *metamorphosis*. The best picture we have of this word in action would be the process a larvae undergoes while transforming into a butterfly, a thing of beauty with more freedom and power than its previous existence afforded.

Most of us learned in our junior high science class that without the struggle of emerging from the cocoon over a long period of time, the butterfly will not become strong enough to fly. The success of its transformation depends upon how well it struggles. So, too, will the success of our leadership in ministry be linked to how well we struggle in the birth of that vision and the growth of the ministry.

Here is the point: You won't arrive at a place of understanding your strengths and style as a leader without a struggle. Developing new perspectives, skills, and ways of leading is a process of trial and error, practice and failure, and even at times weakness turned to strength. Finding the ministry role that suits your natural strengths and style doesn't occur automatically. It takes work, adjustments, adaptations, and realignment over time and ultimately is a reflection of your own spiritual journey in which learning, growth, and change never end. Be willing to do the work to find the role that best suits God's design in your life, and don't be surprised when he brings people and circumstances into your life to build your strengths even greater.

Common Leadership Wisdom: Every ministry leader has natural preferences when it comes to strengths and styles in the ministry.

The Tilt: God constantly develops a leader's strengths and style for the ministry through a process of constant transformation and alignment.

Transformation occurs from the inside out, beginning within the core of our being and resulting in a complete change, leaving nothing untouched in the process. Most important, transformation does not occur without struggle.

Transformation cannot be initiated, effected, or completed by human instrumentality. Each of us is a handcrafted work of divine origin. This is clearly seen in the five factors that take shape and mature as we struggle toward spiritual maturity. These definitions were developed by Rick Warren and have become an international standard of sorts, giving people a common vocabulary to talk about God's unique design built into each of us:

- **S**piritual gifts—A set of special abilities God has given you in order to serve others and share his love.
- Heart—The special passions God has given you so that you can glorify him on earth.
- Abilities—The set of talents God gave you when you were born, which he also wants you to use to make an impact for him.

- Personality—The special way God wired you to navigate life and fulfill your unique Kingdom Purpose.
- Experiences—Those parts of your past, both positive and painful, that God intends to use in great ways.

Understanding our design is important. Not just because we need to give ourselves time to struggle through those things in life and ministry that will prepare us for victory, but because if we are struggling through in a way that does not reflect who God has designed us to be, we will be working against his design and thus not struggling well at all. We need to work at transforming into that unique calling and purpose God has shaped into each one of us when he created us! Better to acknowledge his design in our efforts than try to become something we think or want to be that may not be who God made us to be. Struggling well begins with understanding God's design in you.

Who Are You, Really?

As you think about the five factors, would you consider yourself knowledgeable about who you are, or would you consider yourself as not having a clear understanding of how God has put you together or designed you in this regard? Having a good understanding of how you are put together means that 80 percent of your leadership role is in alignment with your God-given design. By the same token, if you spend the majority of your time on responsibilities that are out of alignment with your strengths, then you will be out of alignment.

A survey of church leaders reveals that 57 percent were not using their God-given strengths on a weekly basis. That places them in the "out of alignment" category. What about you? As you think about your own leadership role, where would you place yourself? Is the idea of understanding your unique design and therefore your unique contribution new to you? Here is a helpful way to gauge how aligned you may be.

Misaligned leaders tend to share these common symptoms:

1. **Frustration in their minds**—When you are asked to serve for long periods of time outside your strengths and passions, you become very frustrated.
2. **Fatigue in their hearts**—If you stay outside your giftedness long enough, your symptoms move from your head to your heart. You will become tired emotionally, spiritually, and relationally because your assignments don't tap into the way God uniquely designed you.
3. **Fear in their lives**—Leaders who stay outside their uniqueness for extended periods of time inevitably move from frustration and fatigue to fear. It is not uncommon to feel you have missed God's plan for your life. Others may fear standing before God and *not* hearing him say, "Well done, good and faithful servant."

God didn't create us to live with frustration, fatigue, and fear. While we may make bad choices that put us in that situation, God doesn't set us up for failure and always provides a way back to satisfaction and fulfillment.

What God *does* intend is for us to understand our uniqueness and serve in the way he created us. Leaders whose roles and responsibilities align with their uniqueness share three common signs or characteristics:

1. **Focus of mind**—Leaders who know their God-given design and have a plan to express it live focused on what the Lord has called them to do. They use the freedom this focus provides to filter opportunities in order to maximize their uniqueness. They are willing to leave some things undone until someone who is designed for this calling steps forward and accepts responsibility to get it done.
2. **Fulfillment of heart**—When leaders continually serve in roles that align with their design, they experience greater joy, fulfillment, and peace. Though their days may be long

and end with fatigue—there is still a smile on their face when they hit the pillow!

3. **Fruitfulness of life**—Whenever leaders use their design to serve God, their skills are sharpened and they bear more fruit, which in turn brings more glory to God, fruit that remains, just as Jesus promised (John 15:16).

If you find yourself identifying with the misaligned descriptions, the challenge to you is to begin the process of understanding your design and then committing to the process of struggling well in the development of your unique contribution. Once you have a good idea of how God has uniquely made you, you need to begin looking for ways to express yourself for his glory. On the other hand, if you find yourself in alignment, then continue to work on your contribution so that your full potential can be realized in whatever you have been called to do in the kingdom.

If you haven't already, now would be a good time for a personal inventory. Take as much time as you need to work your way prayerfully and thoughtfully through this information. Check everything that best describes you. You will compile a profile that will help reveal your unique design. Then you can use these new insights about your life to define your ministry "sweet spot," which will maximize who God has made you to be. As you go, ask God to help you see the outline of the masterpiece he is creating in you. Ask him to reveal his heart's desire for your service to others. Pray that he will show you his path to become the leader you were created to be.

Your Spiritual Gifts

Let's use the following short list of New Testament gifts to identify those you feel God has given you. Not one of these gifts is better than any other. Rather, they demonstrate the need in this world for a wide variety of leaders.

If you truly don't find fulfillment and fruitfulness in a certain type of ministry, don't check the box just because you think you should. Your design is not about who you *should* be. This is a discovery of who you *are*. Senior leaders who are tired of leading because they don't really have the gift of leadership are legion! What they really want to do, for example, is use their gifts to counsel others who are hurting. The key to finding and fulfilling your unique God-given purpose is to be willing to be whoever you discover God has made you to be!

- ❏ **ADMINISTRATION**—(1 Corinthians 12:28) The God-given special ability to serve and strengthen the body of Christ by effectively organizing resources and people in order to efficiently reach ministry goals.
- ❏ **APOSTLESHIP**—(1 Corinthians 12:28) The God-given special ability to serve and strengthen the body of Christ by launching and leading new ministry ventures that advance God's purposes and expand his kingdom. The original Greek meaning of the word is "sent one" (literally, one sent with authority or as an ambassador).
- ❏ **DISCERNMENT**—(1 Corinthians 12:10) The God-given special ability to serve and strengthen the body of Christ by recognizing truth or error within a message, person, or event.
- ❏ **ENCOURAGEMENT**—(Romans 12:8) The God-given special ability to serve and strengthen the body of Christ by helping others live God-centered lives through inspiration, encouragement, counseling, and empowerment.
- ❏ **EVANGELISM**—(Ephesians 4:11-14) The God-given special ability to serve and strengthen the body of Christ by sharing the love of Christ with others in a way that draws them to respond by accepting God's free gift of eternal life.
- ❏ **FAITH**—(1 Corinthians 12:9) The God-given special ability to serve and strengthen the body of Christ by stepping out in faith in order to see God's purposes accomplished, trusting him to handle any and all obstacles along the way.

❏ **GIVING**—(Romans 12:8) The God-given special ability to serve and strengthen the body of Christ by joyfully supporting and funding various kingdom initiatives through material contributions beyond the tithe.

❏ **HELPING**—(Romans 12:7-8) The God-given special ability to serve and strengthen the body of Christ by offering others assistance in reaching goals that glorify God and strengthen the body of Christ.

❏ **HOSPITALITY**—(Romans 12:13) The God-given special ability to serve and strengthen the body of Christ by providing others with a warm and welcoming environment for fellowship.

❏ **KNOWLEDGE**—(1 Corinthians 12:8) The God-given special ability to serve and strengthen the body of Christ by communicating God's truth to others in a way that promotes justice, honesty, and understanding. This gift focuses on the study, learning, and research that equip you to communicate with deep understanding and insight.

❏ **LEADERSHIP**—(Romans 12:8) The God-given special ability to serve and strengthen the body of Christ by casting vision, stimulating spiritual growth, applying strategies, and achieving success where God's purposes are concerned.

❏ **MERCY**—(Romans 12:8) The God-given special ability to serve and strengthen the body of Christ by ministering to those who suffer physically, emotionally, spiritually, or relationally. The actions of those with this gift are characterized by love, care, compassion, and kindness toward others.

❏ **PASTORING**—(Ephesians 4:11-12) The God-given special ability to serve and strengthen the body of Christ by taking spiritual responsibility for a group of believers and equipping them to live Christ-centered lives. *Shepherding* is another word used for this particular gift.

❏ **TEACHING**—(1 Corinthians 12:28) The God-given special ability to serve and strengthen the body of Christ by teaching sound doctrine in relevant ways, empowering people to gain a well-grounded and mature spiritual education. This gift focuses on the unique ability to teach effectively whether the material is your own or someone else's.

❏ **WISDOM**—(1 Corinthians 12:8) The God-given special ability to serve and strengthen the body of Christ by making wise decisions and counseling others with sound advice, all in accordance with God's will.

What would you say are your top three spiritual gifts? How much of your current role in ministry uses these gifts? Are they used sometimes, regularly, or most of the time?

When these questions were posed to Gabe, an executive pastor, he said less than 20 percent of his roles matched his giftedness. He was able to lead organizationally, but he had no outlet to express his spiritual gift of teaching. He loved to share God's word from the pulpit, but was given the opportunity to do this only twice a year, leaving him depressed and defeated. I reminded him that a delay in the opportunity to express his giftedness was not a denial of the gift. It might just be a sign that God was not yet ready for him to use that gift.

Your Heart

God has given each of us a unique *emotional* "heartbeat" that races when we encounter certain leadership roles, subjects, and activities and slows way down when we encounter others. We instinctively gravitate toward those things that ignite our passions. Have you discovered yours yet?

For example, I love casting vision and then designing the strategic plan to get there. But ask me to manage the plan, and we will have problems! I don't love the job of managing and have found that when I try it, the frustration levels rise in me and in those around me. When it comes to maximizing my leadership passions, I love engaging new challenges and finding new codes to crack. My friend Al, on the other hand, loves to lead the team down the field toward victory. He loves putting feet to other people's vision. Al does *not* love casting vision or even setting the goals. If you asked Al to be a visionary leader, his level of joy would drop significantly

As you think about how God wired you, develop your own list, with one column for "Passion Builders" and one for "Passion Busters"—things that cause your emotional heart rate to increase, or decrease, respectively. This information will be useful in preparing you for sharing your ministry with others.

Passion Builders	Passion Busters
1.	1.
2.	2.
3.	3.
4.	4.
5.	5.

Your Abilities

The Bible teaches that, at the moment we accept God's free gift of eternal life through Christ, we are also given our spiritual gifts. Like any gift, we have to unwrap it and put these gifts to use or they will just gather dust. God also gave us natural abilities we can use to bring glory to his name. Do you know your natural abilities? Do you get to express them within your ministry?

One of the quickest ways to determine how you are currently using the abilities God has given you is to review your responsibilities and answer these three questions:

- What roles within your ministry do you *love* doing? These are the things you could do daily—from coaching to counseling, from data entry to designing strategic plans, from speaking to sorting. There are hundreds of different types of abilities.

The goal is to identify and grasp those that bring you the greatest fulfillment and bring God the greatest results.

- What roles within your ministry do you *like* doing? These are the things you can do, but don't necessarily love doing.
- What roles within your ministry could you live *without* doing? These are the things that bring more frustration than fulfillment into your leadership.

The things that you can live without are always things someone else loves to do. Again, it's not about one thing being better than the other. Rather, it's how God designed the body of Christ to operate—interdependent with one another.

At a church in Greenville, Indiana, a move into a new building brought a sudden and urgent need for all kinds of ministries they'd never experienced before the move. The pastor of ministries observed that motivation to meet these needs was high among the membership during that time. So in order to help members get involved in ministry right away, the church developed what they call First Saturdays—a day in which anyone, from individuals to small groups, can come and try out a service opportunity.

The point here is that sometimes we have to try a few things before we know just where and how God wants us to serve. As you're looking over your gifts and abilities, be willing to say yes to God in a few areas that might seem new or strange to you. God has a way of surprising us with answers we'd never have guessed on our own.

Your Personality

Personality, or temperament as some like to call it, is partly genetics and partly development through socialization and enculturation as we grow up. By the time we are thirty years of age or so, only about 5 percent of our behavior can change without some sort of intervention.

Personality acts like an outgoing filter that puts a spin on everything we say and do, creating the person other people experience when we are with them. Since we all tend to be largely unaware of how we come across to others, it is very helpful to get a handle on our personality. Personality is as much a gift to us from God as other aspects of our design and will give us clues to our best use in ministry.

Here is a fun exercise that will help illustrate how information about your personality can be useful. On each scale put an "X" on the line to the left or right of center, depending upon whether you believe you are closer to the descriptive labels on either end. The farther from the center your mark, the more like the label you believe you are. Evenly balanced is not an option, though you may be close. That means you cannot choose to place your "X" exactly in the middle.

Understanding Your Personality

On each scale put an "X" somewhere along the continuum between the pair of descriptive labels. The farther from the center your mark, the more like the label you believe you are. Try not to place your "X" exactly in the middle.

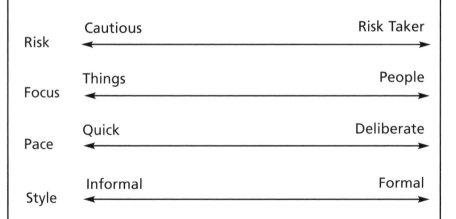

	Cautious	Risk Taker
Risk	◄─────────────────────────────►	

	Things	People
Focus	◄─────────────────────────────►	

	Quick	Deliberate
Pace	◄─────────────────────────────►	

	Informal	Formal
Style	◄─────────────────────────────►	

From *Tilt: Small Shifts in Leadership That Make a Big Difference* © 2010 by Erik Rees and Jeff Jernigan. Used by permission.

Once you have done this, make a list of your predominant qualities. Let's say you are a slightly risk-taking, very people-focused and quick-paced, rather formal individual. Does the role you serve in ministry require these traits? No job fit is perfect, but a bad fit promises a certain amount of fatigue, disappointment, and frustration. Here is a good way to tell: Return to the chart above and put a circle or large dot on each line at the point where you think your job requires you to be. Is there a big difference, or are you close enough?

Your Experiences

Our past affects who we are today and can help point to a future direction. The key is not to live in the past, but learn to leverage the past for God's glory. This reality helps us view even negative experiences in the past with some degree of objectivity. If Paul was right when he said God can use everything in our lives for good purpose (Romans 8:28), then our past has purpose. Each experience has a weight and direction to it that, when taken together, can give us clues to our design.

As you think about your past, what are a few events (positive or painful) that have shaped you into the person you are today? After you have identified a few of them, think about how they have affected you. Here is an example to get you started. Make sure you look for the positive outcome of your experiences.

Using Your Experiences as Strengths

Write down a few events (positive or painful) that have shaped you into the person you are today. What positive lessons or qualities have you gained from those experiences?

Experience	Benefit
Father died when I was a teenager	Learned to be independent
Had a part-time job in high school	Bought and rebuilt an old car
Moved around a lot as a child	Learned to make friends easily
Set a 100-meter-dash state record	Hard work paid off
Got fired from my first job	Learned that stupidity has a price

Your experiences will give you clues to skills, talents, perspectives, attitudes, and vocational aptitudes that all have a built-in direction.

Taken altogether, what do your experiences seem to equip you to be or do?

Now look at the benefits—is there a pattern here? What great lessons! Independent and friendly, this person is industrious, hardworking, and knows the value of thinking things through before acting. (I really did get fired—one of the most unpleasant and at the same time beneficial experiences of my life!) Now, it is your turn. It is easier to see a pattern if you divide your life into ages. You may want to do this on a separate piece of paper. There is no magic number. Simply record enough information over a long enough period of time that a positive pattern begins to emerge.

From *Tilt: Small Shifts in Leadership That Make a Big Difference* © 2010 by Erik Rees and Jeff Jernigan. Used by permission.

Age	Experience	Benefit
6–10 years	1. 2. 3.	1. 2. 3.
11–15	1. 2. 3.	1. 2. 3.
16–20	1. 2. 3.	1. 2. 3.
21–25	1. 2. 3.	1. 2. 3.
26–30	1. 2. 3.	1. 2. 3.
31–35	1. 2. 3.	1. 2. 3.
36–40	1. 2. 3.	1. 2. 3.
41–50	1. 2. 3.	1. 2. 3.
51–60	1. 2. 3.	1. 2. 3.

From *Tilt: Small Shifts in Leadership That Make a Big Difference* © 2010 by Erik Rees and Jeff Jernigan. Used by permission.

Your experiences will give you clues to skills, talents, perspectives, attitudes, and vocational aptitudes that all have a built-in direction.

Taken altogether, what do your experiences seem to equip you to be or do?

Your Style

Leadership takes on many forms. Coaching, mentoring, directing, influencing, facilitating, and encouraging are ways of describing a leadership style. Some people lead from the strength of their personality. This would be called charismatic leadership.

Some people lead best from a well-defined position in an organization, while others are more effective leading from a foundation of rules or guidelines. These are ways of describing how we use authority in the context of any given leadership style. For example, are we charismatic, authoritative, participative, administrative, jurisprudent, or spiritual in our leadership style?

We can obviously lead from many different perspectives, depending upon the circumstance and need. However, each of us has a natural preference when it comes to exercising authority in concert with our style. The exercise of authority is a fundamental description of leadership. How that authority is exercised will look different and be experienced by others differently depending upon our style. What is most natural for you? How are you designed to best operate as a leader based upon God's design in you?

Authentic leadership means simply leading in your sweet spot with the style and use of authority most natural to you. Knowing your sweet spot allows you to deviate from it to other styles when the circumstances require you to exercise authority differently. Knowing your sweet spot also enables you to distinguish between a need for leadership and a need for management in every situation. Manage things. Lead people. If you try to manage people, you will run them off. Not only that, but trying to lead from a style that is alien to whom God made you to be is a sure-fire formula for frustration and failure. On the other hand, following God's lead and identifying your natural style will help open the door to satisfaction and fulfillment.

So, is management a bad thing? Of course not! Ask yourself a simple question: What am I happier doing, working with things or with people? Obviously, working with things requires working with people, but it is the *nature* of the work in focus in this discussion. Here is a case in point:

Working for a number of years in industry as an electrical engineer taught me a lot about myself. For example, I wasn't as excited about getting things done as I was excited about helping the people who worked for me to be successful. It took more effort and concentration for me to create the plant maintenance schedule than it took effort to come alongside a group of electricians and help them solve the problem they were working on. A cup of coffee with a colleague was more personally rewarding to me than reading blueprints and schematics and discovering something everyone else had missed.

What would you say was my natural preference when it came to working with schedules, drawings, and things or working with people and what helped them? Clearly, the nature of the work I enjoyed most involved a relational dimension I wasn't experiencing with tasks that did not involve people. Gifted managers can also be very relational, but the nature of the work they enjoy most involves directing or controlling the use of something. The distinction between leadership and management drawn here is a bit artificial to make a point. Good leaders do manage and good managers do lead, but understanding the difference is important to success in ministry. Here is an illustration of why this is true:

Don was a missionary for ten years in Guatemala. He and his wife worked for a mission organization as part of a team planting churches. Don's job was primarily involved with the operational support of the team and the schools, Bible studies, ministry groups, and churches they worked among. Very detail-oriented, very conscientious, and very directive in his charismatic leadership style, Don mostly gave orders. He was a great manager and very successful. When health reasons brought the family back to America, Don felt led of the Lord to start a new church in his community.

The first five years were great! The challenges of getting a new church off the ground were highly operational in manner and the limited resources available very easy to manage. People responded well to direction from someone who knew what they were doing. At first, relationships to be maintained were few in number. Don liked this since he was an introvert by nature and, though very personable, preferred a very small social circle. Eventually the church grew in size beyond what Don could manage through the exercise of overt control or direct authoritative relationships. The needs of the church were changing operationally as well. There was a staff now that needed leadership (not management), development, training, and relationship. The growing congregation wasn't satisfied with just seeing Don in the pulpit on Sundays and other official occasions, but wanted to relate to him as a real person.

You can imagine Don's frustration and fatigue as the years went by. His gifts as a manager were becoming less and less effective in a ministry that needed more and more leadership. Operations grew beyond his ability to control, and people responded less to dictatorial efforts to maintain control. Sure, Don could have shifted his emphasis to leadership over management. But this would have been only a temporary solution because by experience and natural preference Don was a charismatic, authoritative manager—someone people enjoyed directing them in the disposition of things—but not so much in relating to them personally. It was time to develop new leadership in the ministry—no reason to step out or burn out—you simply raise up those alongside who have the gifts and calling the ministry requires based upon the people you serve.

Sadly, this didn't happen. In a peer-review process, Don was given the feedback that he was not a leader and his lack of leadership was behind many of the challenges the church faced. Two weeks later he stepped down, burned out by swimming upstream for years operating outside his sweet spot. He has not returned to ministry to this day—a great loss to the kingdom.

Here is the fundamental question you need to answer:

Are you a natural leader with management abilities, or a natural manager with leadership abilities?

To help you fully embrace who you are, please take advantage of the online strengths assessment available at www.ser vingsweetspot.com. The thirty-minute assessment you'll find there will help you refine and refocus your God-given strengths and passions. The assessment code for you to use is "TILT." It is important, no matter how you achieve this, that you have a good understanding of your style and authority if you are going to be an authentic leader.

PART II

EMPOWERING OTHERS TO LEAD

CHAPTER SEVEN

Releasing Your Team to Lead

By yourself you're unprotected. With a friend you can face the worst.
Can you round up a third? A three-stranded rope isn't easily snapped.
—*Ecclesiastes 4:12* The Message

Success is a team effort.

For the 1992 Summer Olympics in Barcelona, Spain, the United States fielded a basketball "dream team." Led by legendary greats Larry Bird, Karl Malone, Michael Jordan, and "Magic" Johnson, the team swept game after game. They beat their first opponent, Angola, by a lopsided 116–48 score and went on to win the gold by beating Croatia with a 32-point margin. They finished with an 8-0 record and, in the minds of many, earned themselves a place in the history books as the greatest collection of talent ever assembled on one team. I recall Chuck Daly talking at the press conference after winning the gold medal about how, together, the team made dreams come true.

How right he was! Coach Daly's thoughts can be a tremendous insight for pastors and church leaders who have caught God's vision for being empowering leaders by building empowering ministries. The writer of Hebrews puts it this way: "Let us consider how we may spur one another on toward love and good deeds. Let us not give up meeting together, as some are in the habit of doing, but let us encourage one another—and all the more as you see the Day approaching" (10:24-25 NIV).

Whatever your passion or dream for ministry, one thing is certain: You can't accomplish it alone—you're not meant to. God is calling you to make sure every member of the body of Christ you serve is a minister, and that goal is beyond the reach of any one of us. Not only that, but ministry is always more fulfilling when you do it with a team. Because we each have different strengths, we can make up for what any single person may lack in gifting, talent, or experience and pull together toward a common goal. God created us to need one another to make his kingdom dream for us come true. His plan for me is to need the help of others and for them to need my help.

If you find yourself not wanting to share your ministry, welcome to the club. When I first confronted what God was calling me to do in ministry—equip others, release them, and give the ministry away—I resisted the call. One excuse after another came to mind of why it was not necessary to share my job with others. How could I trust people I barely knew with my dream? But I did find it easy to share with those with whom I had the greatest relationships. As I look back on my ministry, I'm so grateful I got out of the way and allowed others to help in places where their giftedness strengthened my weakness. Our greatest example in this is God himself. The Trinity ascribes different roles to God as Father, Son, and Holy Spirit, yet they are all God! Equal value, different roles . . . sort of like a ministry team. Ministry is a plural activity. It always has been.

So as you think about building a team of people, start to think about those you trust most and already have a relationship with. Then challenge each person you invite to your team to own a part of the ministry so you can fulfill your purpose and each of them can start to find and fulfill his or hers. This isn't about nepotism, but about using the power of networking to realize your dream. As you invite people you trust, they'll begin inviting people they trust. The end result: Your goal is accomplished.

If you are going to become an empowering leader and build an empowering ministry, you must build your own "dream team" to champion and support your ministry vision. Creating it will allow you to work within your sphere of ministry (your God-given design and purpose) while you empower and encourage them to do the same.

To help him advance his mission, Jesus himself built a ministry dream team: "Jesus went up on a mountain and called out the ones he wanted to go with him. And they came to him. Then he appointed twelve of them and called them his apostles. They were to accompany him, and he would send them out to preach, giving them authority to cast out demons" (Mark 3:13-15 NLT).

Jesus knew God's kingdom would be more effectively advanced if he multiplied his vision through a group of close associates. In fact, he saw gathering his dream team as an essential part of his mission. It was so important that before he had even gone to the cross, before he had risen from the dead, Jesus told his heavenly Father he had finished the work God had given him to do: "I have brought you glory on earth by completing the work you gave me to do. . . . I have revealed you to those whom you gave me out of the world. . . . Now they know that everything you have given me comes from you. For I gave them the words you gave me and they accepted them" (John 17:4-8a NIV).

Jesus knew his time on earth would be brief and was quickly coming to an end. If his work in building God's kingdom was going to continue beyond what he could personally accomplish on earth, he needed to recruit a team. He believed so deeply in the importance of assembling the right team that he spent the entire night in prayer before he announced whom he had chosen (Luke 6:12).

If the Son of God needed a "dream team" for his ministry vision to be fulfilled, there's no doubt you need a team to succeed as well.

Common Leadership Wisdom: Impact in ministry requires a strong leader supported by team members.

The Tilt: Impact in ministry requires a leader able to release team members for maximum effectiveness.

Some will not be happy about the implications. They may think to themselves *Why do I need people in my life? Asking people for help is a sign of weakness. I can do it on my own.* We need to take to heart that this is contrary to God's design for ministry, for us individually, and recognize it as a defensive position that really protects us from what we consciously or unconsciously fear the most. Perhaps you are the kind of disciplined and talented individual who really can do it on your own to some extent. Hear this clearly: This is not God's best for you and not his best for your ministry.

The Bible clearly says we need one another: "By yourself you're unprotected. With a friend you can face the worst. Can you round up a third? A three-stranded rope isn't easily snapped" (Ecclesiastes 4:12 *The Message*). The truth is, we need people who know us well enough to encourage us, challenge us, and confront us—right when we need it most. Without that kind of personal relationship, we would harbor secrets Satan could use to discourage and defeat us. We also need close ministry relationships, because if we don't share our ministry with others, we are weakening the body of Christ.

So, this may be the moment when you have to admit that you don't have the personal and ministry support team you need to succeed. I'm thankful for the way my life and ministry changed once I acknowledged my need for a team to champion and challenge me and to extend the reach of the ministry God had in mind. I never would have imagined that asking people to join me in ministry would bring such release and replenishment to my spirit.

God wants to meet our deepest needs through relationships. He designed us so that we would experience life to its fullest only when we live and work in community. Working on a team is harder than going it alone. It's hard for many of us to give up control. We find it hard to trust people who may not have the experience we have. We believe the job isn't going to get done right unless we do it ourselves. But not only is there too much for one person to do, God's plan is that the only way to experience the best he has to offer is for us to work as a team, even when others are hard to work with. James 3:18 says: "You can develop a healthy, robust community that lives right with God and enjoy its results only if you do the hard work of getting along with each other, treating each other with dignity and honor" (*The Message*).

The idea that ministry is a team challenge is built into the Scripture itself. Romans 12:4-5 tells us: "Just as there are many parts to our bodies, so it is with Christ's body. We are all parts of it, and it takes every one of us to make it complete, for we each have different work to do. So we belong to each other, and each needs all the others" (TLB). No one person has what it takes to do everything that is needed in the ministry. We need one another. We ought, therefore, to be intentional about the way in which we construct our teams.

Scripture also reveals that teams can accomplish far more than individuals working by themselves. Ecclesiastes 4:9-12 says: "Two are better off than one, because together they can work more effectively. If one of them falls down, the other can help him up. But if someone is alone and falls, it's just too bad, because there is no one to help him. If it is cold, two can sleep together and stay warm, but how can you keep warm by yourself? Two people can resist an attack that would defeat one person alone. A rope of three cords is hard to break" (GNT).

When Jesus sent his disciples out to minister, he sent them in pairs. Some commentators believe the intent of this passage may indicate "two twos" or four people going together. Jesus knew that effective ministry requires the encouragement and support of others. Ministry can get extremely difficult. People become discouraged. When we organize ourselves in teams, we have strength that none of us would have individually. That's why Nehemiah organized the Israelites by groups and families when they were rebuilding the walls of Jerusalem. Half of them stood guard while the other half worked. Together, they accomplished what they were failing to do as individuals.

Removing Constraints

Releasing your team to lead is going to take more than just an understanding of the importance of teamwork and a commitment to team building. You are going to have to think differently about your role as a team leader. You are the releasing agent, the one who opens the gates, the remover of constraints that those in ministry believe restrain them from achieving the goals that have been agreed upon. A constraint is the weakest point, the most significant obstacle, the bottleneck, the impediment to moving forward with the vision you and your team have all bought into. To some extent, each team member will have to address these constraints individually, but here comes the tilt: Overcoming and removing constraints is primarily the responsibility of the team leader. (That would be you.)

Four kinds of human factor constraints typically impede progress in ministry: administrative, policy, philosophical, or ideological. The impact of these constraints is to act as a governor, controlling the pace at which everything else happens or holding things up altogether. Ultimately, constraints determine the level of performance of your ministry.

Administrative Constraints exist when there are no progress reports, no monitoring of performance, and no use of indicators to track progress in a way that enables you to maintain both a strategic perspective and a situational awareness of what is going on in the ministry. These kinds of constraints are illustrated by statements like:

"Why can't we control overtime?"

"There is no focus on training and development in this ministry."

"There is no relationship between operational expense and the budget."

"Where are we in the strategic plan right now?"

Policy Constraints exist when current policies or practice (unwritten policy) impedes or prevents progress. Some structure and guidelines are needed in every ministry organization, so the answer isn't clearing the decks and forging ahead without direction or controls. Policy constraints should always be evaluated carefully and may need to stay in place. These kinds of constraints are illustrated by statements like:

"We've never done it that way before."
"The system won't let us do that."
"That's not the way we do it here."
"That violates policy or procedure."

Philosophical Constraints exist when values, attitudes, or beliefs are in opposition to progress. This can be represented as a lack of alignment with ministry goals, a lack of understanding of the vision, or unproductive attitudes that prevail in key players or groups. These kinds of constraints are illustrated by statements like:

"We need to focus on our own folks and not on evangelism."
"This ministry has done nothing for me!"
"Those people don't know what they are doing."
"There is no leadership around here!"

Ideological Constraints exist in the form of doctrines or opinions of individuals or groups. They are recognized as paradigms or mind-sets that prevent change or progress. These constraints are illustrated by statements like:

"It's not just a 'we-they' attitude, it's us and the enemy!"
"We don't like change around here."
"The values we have are not the ones we need."
"If it didn't originate with us, it's not a good idea."

These are the kinds of things your team needs to be released from in order to pursue what God has called all of you to do together. Facing these constraints will be a process that takes time and will require of you transformational leadership. You are the key to releasing your team. It may be easy sometimes to believe that the holdup you may be experiencing is one or more anchors on your team. My friend, you are the gatekeeper. Removing obstacles for your team is in your job description, not theirs.

The Heart of Community

More than four hundred years ago, the poet John Donne wrote, "No man is an island"—and that truth has not changed. God has custom-designed us to live best in community. Community is the crucible in which dealing successfully with constraints is worked out. This means we must engage others, request help from others, and win others to the task of completing the unique work God has planned for us. Though the responsibility is yours, you are not expected to do it alone.

The foundation for this kind of working together in Christian community is the utterly unique concept of *agape* love. If self-sacrificing, others-centered, God-honoring love is not at the center of our ministry relationships, we will never experience the empowerment God desires to give us. Without this kind of love, we cannot empower others, either.

When several religious teachers challenged Jesus to identify the most important commandment in the Bible, he said the first and greatest was to " 'love the Lord your God with all your heart and with all your soul and with all your mind and with all your strength.' The second [command] is this: 'Love your neighbor as yourself.' There is no commandment greater than these" (Mark 12:30-31 NIV). The deeper our love for God grows, the more it spills over into other lives as he fills us with his agape love.

Our desire to shower others with God-motivated love is

driven by our own experience of being transformed by God's love. The Bible says, "Dear friends, since God so loved us, we also ought to love one another. No one has ever seen God; but if we love one another, God lives in us and his love is made complete in us" (1 John 4:11-12 NIV).

No matter how much we may wish we could play the Lone Ranger, there is no escaping the fact that God created us to do life together. The Bible says, "Let us consider how we may spur one another on toward love and good deeds. Let us not give up meeting together, as some are in the habit of doing, but let us encourage one another—and all the more as you see the Day approaching" (Hebrews 10:24-25 NIV). When our ministry relationships are motivated by love, the rewards are impossible to enumerate.

When the Apostle Paul wrote the "Love Chapter"— 1 Corinthians 13—he was teaching all of us what love looks like at every level, in every area of our lives. Listen to what he said about the characteristics and rewards of love: "Love is patient, love is kind. It does not envy, it does not boast, it is not proud. It is not rude, it is not self-seeking, it is not easily angered, it keeps no record of wrongs. Love does not delight in evil but rejoices with the truth. It always protects, always trusts, always hopes, always perseveres" (vv. 4-7 NIV).

God's desire for your ministry is that you serve with a group of people who are patient with you and treat you with kindness, with whom you do not need to compete, who are not boastful about themselves but are proud of you, who are not rude to you and not easily angered by what you do, who do not hold your past against you but rather help you live by the truth of God's word. What a wonderful list of rewards. We don't deserve any of it, but by the inexpressible grace of God, these rewards are ours.

The Bible says, "Accept one another, then, just as Christ accepted you, in order to bring praise to God" (Romans 15:7 NIV). When our ministry teams live in a community of love, we experience the blessing of complete acceptance, affirmation, and appreciation from those with whom we work. Our team members encourage us and confront us in love when we wander off course. We are constantly encouraged and challenged as we strive to live with and for God—together. Even the Lone Ranger, I was recently reminded, had his trusting teammate Tonto.

Godly Advice

One of the most valuable benefits of ministering in a community of love is the wisdom God shares with us through the counsel of godly advisers. All of us trust our own instincts and opinions far more than we should. Proverbs 14:12 says, "There is a way that seems right to a man, but in the end it leads to death" (NIV). Proverbs 15:22 adds: "Plans go wrong for lack of advice; many advisers bring success" (NLT). The simple fact is, as the Lord declares, "My thoughts are not your thoughts, neither are your ways my ways" (Isaiah 55:8 NIV). We need to hear the wisdom of God that he communicates to us through others, especially when it comes to matters of ministry.

When you share your ministry dreams and plans with your team before you become emotionally attached to them, you receive the benefit of your team's impartiality and understanding of your blind spots. You will discover that God will speak to you through those relationships. Because we operate in a community of grace and love, you can trust them.

God's greatest empowerment for your ministry will be realized as you build a team that operates in such a community. As difficult as it may be to accept what they have to say sometimes, you must be willing to listen and change your course when God speaks to you through your team. When you do, you will not only be able to discern what is worth investing your resources in, but you will also have the privilege of bringing God's dreams into reality. Often your team will have the insights you need to be that lifter of constraints they need. The end result is a ministry vision that honors God, rather than your own desires.

Your Dream Team Roster

Imagine your team is ready to take the field at the next Olympic Games. The crowd is going wild as the announcer's voice echoes the names and positions of each player on your ministry dream team. All that's left is to win the gold.

We're going to finalize that roster now. As you fill in the blanks below, you will be defining your team, clarifying the role of each member on the team, and identifying how each one's design strengthens the team.

Player Profile:

Starting at: _____ (role) from _____

(town) is _____

(name), who strengthens the team by (strengths)

_____

_____

and will champion the following areas (responsibilities):

_____

_____

Player Profile:

Starting at: _____ (role) from _____

(town) is _____

(name), who strengthens the team by (strengths)

_____

_____

and will champion the following areas (responsibilities):

_____

_____

Player Profile:
Starting at: _____ (role) from _____
(town) is _____
(name), who strengthens the team by (strengths)

_____

_____

and will champion the following areas (responsibilities):

_____

_____

Player Profile:
Starting at: _____ (role) from _____
(town) is _____
(name), who strengthens the team by (strengths)

_____

_____

and will champion the following areas (responsibilities):

_____

_____

Player Profile:
Starting at: _____ (role) from _____
(town) is _____
(name), who strengthens the team by (strengths)

_____

_____

and will champion the following areas (responsibilities):

_____

_____

Player Profile:

Starting at: _____ (role) from _____

(town) is _____

(name), who strengthens the team by (strengths)

_____

_____

and will champion the following areas (responsibilities):

_____

_____

From *Tilt: Small Shifts in Leadership That Make a Big Difference* © 2010 by Erik Rees and Jeff Jernigan. Used by permission.

A word of caution about putting your dream team together and working to make them successful: As a leader, your role is ensuring team members have the resources they need, the support from you they need in removing constraints, and the direction and leadership from you that they need. Never make it about you. It should be about "us" when it comes to the dream team. Here is a true story about someone who never got a dream team off the ground because he made it about him and his career.

Max is the senior pastor of a medium-sized church in Arizona. My friend Larry and his wife, Marie, had just moved to town and started attending Max's church. Larry is a very successful businessman who works because he likes to, not because he has to. He and Marie are financially secure and very generous. Moreover, they have been involved in ministry for years, leading Bible studies, modeling evangelism, creating small groups—an ideal couple with time on their hands most people would welcome to their ministry!

Larry made an appointment to meet with Max for lunch one day after having been at the church for nearly four months. At lunch Larry shared his testimony, his and Marie's experience in ministry, and asked Max where he could use volunteers. They were both willing to serve anywhere. Any pastor in his right mind would do double backflips for this kind of couple! Volunteering to do anything? Experienced in ministry? Generous with their financial support, too? What a package! Most of us lie awake at night praying for these kinds of God-sends! Talk about a candidate for the dream team!

When Max heard that Larry had a lot of experience with Purpose Driven Church® models, he sat back in his chair and frowned. Noticing the expression on his face, Larry stopped talking. Max began to explain that the last pastor had gotten himself fired by the deacon board after trying to bring Purpose Driven® ministry (a church health model pioneered by Saddleback Church) into the church, and he wouldn't touch it with a ten-foot pole. Then, instead of encouraging Larry and Marie to plug in where they could serve, Max told them they should move on and find another church! True story!

Max had a vision that Larry was excited about. Larry and Marie sat in church all those weeks listening and praying about what part God would want them to have as a resource to Max in bringing that vision to fruition. Now they had no choice but to leave. Here is the problem: On the surface it seems that Max is afraid Larry's heart for purpose-driven ministry will cause trouble in the church. Below the surface, though, Max is being even more self-protective. As it turns out, Larry actually has more successful ministry experience in life than does Max. Max doesn't want Larry around to show him up, make him look bad, or steal any of his thunder.

Too bad. I have known Larry a long time. Long enough to know that no matter how inexperienced or insecure Max may have been, Larry would have been only a blessing to him and to the ministry. Larry would graciously avoid competition, support Max, make him look good and not bad, and never ever steal the limelight. Max, in being self-protective about his career, has nearly guaranteed he will never live out his vision. Max has just driven away the one couple best suited to helping achieve his goals for the ministry. Instead of bringing them on board for a period of time to observe performance and develop relationships while asking God to confirm in each of their hearts joining the team on a more permanent basis, Max made a decision based more on his own personal future than that of the ministry.

Don't do that!

Challenge Me!

Once your team members are in place, you need to take one final step so they truly can play a key role in seeing your kingdom dream come true. You must give them *permission* to challenge you by speaking truth into your life.

The Bible dares us to welcome wisdom: "Above all and before all, do this: Get Wisdom! Write this at the top of your list: Get Understanding!" (Proverbs 4:7 *The Message*). Getting wisdom happens only when you intentionally seek it and ask for it. Could you benefit from having people speak the truth in love to you? If so, please accept the challenge and give people permission to cheer for you, challenge you, and correct you for God's glory. The Bible says the results will come when we work hard: "You can develop a healthy, robust community that lives right with God and enjoy its results only if you do the hard work of getting along with each other, treating each other with dignity and honor" (James 3:18 *The Message*).

Once you have prayed for, pursued, and placed your dream team members, the next step toward becoming an empowering leader is to identify the constraints to be removed from the path ahead. This will become part of your empowering ministry message that will mobilize your members into ministry.

CHAPTER EIGHT

Releasing Your Members to Serve

All who are called can receive the eternal inheritance God has promised them. —Hebrews 9:15 NLT

For a party to be successful, everyone has to receive an invitation. The size of your invitation determines the size of your vision. In the fall of 2004, we witnessed the most amazing ministry project either of us had ever seen when our church committed itself to feeding all the homeless people in our county—three meals a day for forty days. When we felt the Lord leading us to tackle that challenge, we had no idea how many homeless there were in our county. Further investigation revealed we were talking about *forty-two thousand people!*

If you have ever organized a major ministry project, you understand what a tremendous challenge we had on our hands. We had to identify hundreds of ministry opportunities and their locations throughout the county, organize effectively according to some priority, communicate them to tens of thousands of people, and recruit more volunteers than the number of people actually attending our weekend services.

But we did it! By God's grace, the project grew even beyond our county, and we were able to connect 23,000 people in 3,000 small groups located in eighty-three cities across Southern California. About 9,200 volunteers collected more than two million pounds of food—the largest drive of its kind in United States history.

Besides sharing the good news of God's love with thousands upon thousands of hungry souls, our members found that God continued to launch them into ministry even after the project was completed. One small group put together and distributed 130 hygiene kits at the Orange County Rescue Mission. Two small groups—one of which had only four members—worked together to assemble twenty-eight care packages for orphaned girls in Iraq. Another six-member group felt God leading them to host a Christmas party for 700 residents of a low-income apartment complex. They recruited fourteen other groups to help and pulled off a successful event, complete with gifts, lunch, a magic show for the kids, and the reading of the Christmas story.

And it didn't stop there. People were energized by serving others, and small-group applications grew well beyond simple direct assistance. The men of one small group were on the way to pick up one of their teammates only to discover when they arrived at his house that he had just dropped dead of a heart attack. Mom was left without insurance and without full-time work, with two boys to raise. Guess what! That small group, representing fourteen families, pulled together the resources *to put those boys through college!* Now that is long-term service that takes staying power and commitment that go well beyond a single event! Talk about releasing your members!

Our awareness of all those ministry needs didn't mean people were automatically going to step forward to help. We *had* to invite them to join us in serving. *Invite, invite, invite, invite*—we cannot say the word often or loud enough! It takes seven to ten "touches" or invitations to get the average person to pay attention, consider the opportunity, and respond one way or the other. Most of us simply invite people once and quit. A touch might be by word of mouth, or an announcement, or a flyer, or a post card snail-mailed or sent electronically; a phone call, an announcement on the radio, or a door hanger left on the front door. We had to *work* hard at being invitational. The same thing is true in your ministry. All your opportunities need to be collected, organized, prioritized, and communicated to the ministry in a way that engages people individually.

Common Leadership Wisdom: We need to encourage our members to serve where needed in the ministry.

The Tilt: We need to release our members to serve wherever God has called and gifted them to serve.

Once you have understood who you are—and aren't—in ministry and gathered around you a "dream team" to collaborate with you, the time has come to give away the ministry so the entire congregation can share the experience of seeing God's "infinitely more" vision become a reality in your community. This idea of giving something away is easier said than done. The process engages all those issues covered in earlier chapters: Why are you in this ministry, what is your motivation, can you release control appropriately, can you share the credit, whom do you serve?

It is not enough to build a great team, mobilize a following, and plant them in your ministry. The harvest is so much bigger than a single ministry. We must empower people to respond to what God has called and gifted them to do inside and outside our own particular team, church, or ministry. When Jesus challenged the disciples to "go" and make disciples (Matthew 28:18-20), there was no institutional church yet. In fact, the idea of "going" has the sense of "as you are going" through life. And get this . . . Jesus tells them to teach everyone what he has commanded including this commission to go make disciples, effectively guaranteeing the reproduction of ministry in all walks of life wherever believers go. This can't happen if we don't empower and release people to serve wherever they find themselves. All of this starts with releasing and empowering them to serve where they are right now.

What's in Your Bucket?

If you were running an employment service, you would need to know where the job opportunities were, and beyond that you'd need to know how "hot," or how current, those opportunities were in reality. The last thing you would want to do is point someone in your ministry in the direction of a nonopportunity, a dead end. Neither do you want a volunteer who's excited to serve to call the ministry leader and hear, "Oh, I'm sorry. We don't need you anymore." That person goes away thinking, *They don't have a place for me.*

We want all our members to feel there's a place for them in ministry. But you can't effectively give away the jobs unless you know what all of them are. So the first step has to be collecting—making a list of the opportunities you have and identifying opportunities that need to be created. Generally speaking, people are not interested in "needs" or "tasks." They're looking for "opportunities." Have you noticed how often you're hearing that word lately? It's the same with volunteers. They don't want to work at a *task* or just fill a *need*. They want to be part of an *opportunity*. They will respond much more readily if you approach them by saying, "Here's a great ministry opportunity for you." Opportunities are much more exciting than needs and tasks. Here's why: Because an opportunity holds the promise of making a difference. Staff person, volunteer, supporter, stranger—it doesn't make a difference. If people know they will experience making a measurable difference, they will get on board. The idea of a task or a need has a sense of invisibility attached to it, something that is just make-work that may not directly contribute to anything.

A great place to begin building your collection of ministry opportunities is with yourself. Remember these three questions: What do you love? What do you like? What can you live without? Taking the time to review your own responsibilities is a great way to start filling your ministry opportunity bucket. At

Saddleback Church, we've found that by asking every one of our staff members and lay leaders these questions, we're able to help them share their ministry with more of our members through the process of identifying what they are not the best at and don't have the time for. Their liability becomes someone else's opportunity.

This isn't a matter of being prideful about our strengths or unwilling to do the unpleasant tasks that need to be done. We're talking about realizing that, of all the responsibilities God has given us, each of us naturally gravitates toward some and not toward others. So creating these lists is a practical exercise in looking at how God designed you, factoring in your ministry "sweet spot," and identifying what you should be doing and what you should be letting others do.

In chapter 6, you answered three questions:

- What parts of your current ministry responsibilities do you love doing?
- What parts of your current ministry responsibilities do you like doing?
- What parts of your current ministry responsibilities could you live without doing?

Ask the other staff members and ministry leaders in your church the same questions. All the items that become listed as "live without" are likely to be someone else's "love to do." Those are great ministry opportunities for your ministry members.

Excitement and vision begin to build when ministry leaders start asking God to bring into the ministry others who can help with the aspects the leaders aren't wired to perform. We're finally admitting God doesn't intend for us to do everything by ourselves and recognizing he has created others who are designed to do those things. Here is a simple test: Ask yourself what you would do if ten volunteers walked in right now and said, "Here I am! How can I help?" What would you ask them to do? Where would you put them to work in your ministries? If we are truly going to release our members into ministry, we must stretch our minds to think of meaningful, credible, and genuinely necessary opportunities for them to participate in. We can't release people into ministry if we have no place for them to go.

Put the Cookies on the Lowest Shelf

Once you have collected your ministry opportunities, the next step is to categorize them. This element is much more significant than it seems on the surface. The act of organizing opportunities affects the way people will see them and the way that you will see the people you will be inviting—and possibly those you will not be inviting. The key is to make your categories clear so that they can be communicated easily. For example, one of the main questions many people have on their minds as they consider volunteer opportunities is *How much does this require of me?* No one wants to commit to a ministry only to discover they are in over their head. Even if a clear profile of each opportunity is provided, organizing them according to the time required and the complexity of the job can be a major help to prospective volunteers.

After we conducted a churchwide survey that indicated "time" was the number one filter our members were looking through when thinking about serving, we developed some categories that acknowledge time as a very precious commodity:

- **Simple Opportunities**
  - Time requirement: 1 hour per week
  - Gifts unknown and untested
  - Skills for specific task/experience helpful
  - General passion to meet a need
  - Seeker/new or young believer
  - Church membership not required
  - Examples: Greeting team, traffic team, landscape team.

- **Stay-at-Home Opportunities**
  - Time requirement: 1–2 hours per week
  - Skills for specific task/experience very helpful
  - General passion to meet a need
  - Church membership required
  - Examples: Data entry team and Internet research team.
- **Strength-based Opportunities**
  - Time requirement: 2–4 hours per week
  - Gifts are developing
  - Passion for ministry
  - Some experience required
  - Stable spiritual growth
  - Examples: Any opportunity that requires a specific passion, gift, or experience. Serving within a support group, for example, is a great way to use your past painful experiences to minister to others.
- **Servant Leader Opportunities**
  - Time requirement: 4+ hours per week
  - Proven gifts and people skills
  - Strong passion/ministry vision
  - Solid spiritual foundation
  - Leadership training completed
  - Examples: Leadership opportunities within ministries, outreaches, Sunday school, and small groups.
- **Seasonal Opportunities**
  - Time requirement: Minimal
  - No experience required
  - Unsure of gifts
  - Church membership not required
  - Examples: Christmas and Easter services general support teams.
- **Short-Term Project**
  - Time requirement: 1–4 weeks
  - No experience required
  - Skills for specific task/experience helpful

- o Church membership required
- o Willingness to serve where needed
- o Examples: Any project that has a dedicated end date.
- **Small-Group Friendly Opportunities**
  - o Time requirement: Various
  - o Willingness to serve where needed
  - o Examples: Any activity in which a group of people can serve together. Christmas services and Easter services offer great group service opportunities.

A good set of categories can lead you to other creative ideas about organizing ministry projects. For example, when one of our team members got to thinking outside the box about "stay-at-home" projects, we came up with the idea of putting something *in* a box! Our "Ministry-In-A-Box" initiative came out of a survey that revealed many of our people would serve two to three hours a week if they could do it during the week from home. So we put projects in a box they can take home and work on there: stuffing envelopes or binders, folding flyers, organizing files, data entry, transcription, making labels, placing phone calls, doing research. They can do these projects on their own, as a family, or as a small group.

We have developed this list from the perspective of a large ministry, either a church, mission organization, or other large Christian enterprise. You can break it down into simpler categories and shorter lists for anything, right down to a small group or Bible study you may be leading. Here is the principle: If you aim at nothing, you will hit it every time. Categorizing opportunities creates *targets* of opportunity, targets that relate to goals that move your endeavors forward rather than activities that produce a lot of heat and motion but no progress. Activity doesn't equate to progress, but the *intentional release* of people focused on specific targets does.

Challenge the Ministry

Once you have collected and categorized your ministry opportunities, the next step is to deliver them to your members. This gives your vision and mission a voice. How will you let your members know about these opportunities? Spend time carefully considering the "voice" that will challenge people to get involved. Knowing your people, choosing the right message for them, and delivering that message in the right way help them make the commitment to serve.

Serving others is at the very heart of the Christian life. The Greatest Commandment (Matthew 22:37-39) tells us to love our neighbors. Jesus made it plain that even he came to serve and not to be served (Matthew 20:28). Most believers genuinely desire to be part of something significant, and you hold in your hands opportunities for them to serve beyond themselves. There's profound significance in that.

A word of caution: We may find it effective in the short run to emphasize the urgency of a need or the fact that people haven't responded, but members who volunteer for those reasons don't last. Leveraging guilt is one of the most common mistakes made in communicating ministry opportunities. Deep, lasting motivation arises when people catch a vision for ministry and give their heart to it, not just their intellect. The battle for the mind is won in the imagination, and imagination is where a well-communicated vision resides.

Another common mistake is failing to make the "ask," as salespeople often say. Like so many nonchurched people who would come to church if someone just asked them, many ministry members are simply waiting to be asked to help with an opportunity that matches their ability and availability. How the challenge is delivered can make a crucial difference in how it is received.

Here is what you need to know in order to effectively "invite" people.

Be receiver-oriented: Know your audience and how to talk to them. Whether Jesus was talking to Nicodemus (a Pharisee trained in the law of Moses) or the Samaritan woman (a person of bad reputation and no education and on the other side of some important social and cultural boundaries), Jesus knew his audience and how to communicate in a manner that got his message across in the most effective way for that individual. The alternative is to be message-oriented, making the invitation all about you and the information you want the audience to get . . . regardless of their filters, perspectives, attitudes, or understandings. It's about getting through to the audience, not about you and not about the information. The message will get through if you are receiver-oriented.

Keep it simple: A complex invitation causes people to stop listening while they try to figure out what is being communicated—or worse, to respond with skepticism, doubt, or distrust. It doesn't matter what the media is—visual, written, auditory, in person, or electronic—the initial invitation must be clear and simple. If people respond, you will have plenty of opportunity to get into the particulars. The simple invitation has the best chance of crossing communication barriers unaffected. Look at one of the most succinct ways of sharing the gospel today: "For God so loved the world, that He gave His only begotten Son, that whoever believes in Him shall not perish, but have eternal life" (John 3:16 NASB). The truth about who Jesus is, what he has done, and the response he desires from us is a simple message with profound results.

Don't apologize: It is easy sometimes to take on an apologetic tone when asking for people to step up and participate in ministry activities. However, an apologetic tone communicates that you are coming to them on the heels of some prior failure to recruit, that you lack a certain degree of sincerity and therefore lack genuineness. Worse, it may communicate that there is something wrong, difficult, or distasteful about what you are asking them to do. Be positive and upbeat. A positive invitation crafted specifically for your audience that states the opportunity clearly and simply wins every time.

Ambition

This may seem like a strange place to bring up the subject of ambition; but once we have recruited and released people to help out with all these needs in the ministry, a few may rise to the surface as real champions. In fact, they may do things far better than we can. They may even be better at doing our job than we are! Here is where ambition can be a rub. Sometimes leaders tend not to recruit people who have the potential for surpassing them because of a fear that they may not be able to control them, or that they may outshine them, or that they may take away their place.

Ambition is not a bad word. It reflects our drive to succeed, to build, to create, to overcome, to establish, and to make a difference for God. But here is the tilt: Ambition indulged for selfish purposes is just another way of saying we have an ego out of control. Rather, we should always want people around us who have the potential of greater success than we can achieve! Here is the secret to keeping ambition out of the way: "Promotion and power come from nowhere on earth, but only from God. He promotes one and deposes another" (Psalm 75:6-7 TLB). If you believe that it is God who places us in positions of leadership and authority, then you have nothing to worry about from someone you perceive as a threat to your position. That person could be ten times more qualified and you are not going to look bad or be replaced if God is the one who put you where you are.

Common Leadership Wisdom: Those who succeed in ministry are ambitious *for the things God has laid on their hearts.*

The Tilt: Those who succeed in ministry are ambitious *for what God has on his heart for* other people.

How Ambitious Are You?

Here are a few questions to help you check your ambition. Each question can be answered simply yes or no.

1. Do you inwardly cringe when someone takes credit for something you accomplished or materially contributed to?
2. Do you join those recognized for their accomplishments, rejoicing and celebrating with them, or do you secretly resent their success and fear being overshadowed or left behind?
3. When you are recognized, do you share the credit?
4. Do you enjoy going to work every day?
5. Is there a sense of moral obligation to the quality of decisions you make?
6. Do these questions make you uncomfortable, preferring to be less vulnerable or transparent even with yourself?
7. Do you acknowledge the accomplishments of your peers and subordinates?
8. If you were to list the things that really energize you, would the list include what the organization you work for has as its mission or goals?
9. Are you really interested in contributing to the improvement of work life where you are?
10. Are you really interested in improving the human condition as an outcome of the product or service you or your company provides?

Excerpted from *The Power of a Loving Man*, Jeffrey T. Jernigan, 2006, B&H Publishers. Used by permission.

From *Tilt: Small Shifts in Leadership That Make a Big Difference* © 2010 by Erik Rees and Jeff Jernigan. Used by permission.

Did anything surprise you in your response? Do your answers suggest an unhealthy ambition? Whose successes are you focused on most of the time? Ask one or two people who know you well to respond to the questions as if they were evaluating you. Do their answers differ from yours? This is a good way to tell if your ambitions are truly for God's desires and glory, or for your own.

The Apostle Paul uses an interesting play on words in 1 Corinthians 12:27-28 to make a point about ambition without ever using the word. He was responding to questions sent to him by the church at Corinth in the midst of controversy and division created largely by ambitious people focused on their own success over that of others. Paul first reminds them that they are all members of Christ's body, the church at large. He has already established that this membership is among equals and that there should be no division among them. Now, he goes on to address the issue of leadership and uses an interesting phrase, "God has appointed in the church . . ." (12:28 NASB), listing some of these roles. The word *appointed* (*tithemi*) means to physically place or put by laying something flat on a horizontal plane or as a metaphor for having equal value. Though our education, experience, gifts, abilities, or calling may set us apart from others, we have been placed alongside them in ministry by God as equals in spite of these differences. Another word for *appointed* not used here is an antonym (*isthemi*) that means to place or put things vertically, stand them up physically, or as a metaphor for having greater value or more authority. There is a reason that word is not used here.

The Apostle Peter in 1 Peter 1:1-7 talks about humility using two different words to describe our role as shepherds. We are to clothe ourselves in *humility* (literally to be modest in our own self-appraisal) in our relationships with one another, and we are to be *humble* (cast down, base, low, and looking up) in considering our selves to be the lesser among equals. When this is the case, it is easy to be ambitious for the things of others and more difficult to be ambitious for our own things.

Get Out of Your Team's Way

Probably the single greatest obstacle you will have to overcome in releasing your members for ministry is you. All these tips about being organized and planning your progress, about the invitation and its simple clarity, are all important. But you can have all these things in place and still fail to recruit, energize, and release people in ways that empower them to take the ministry further than you ever could if your ambition gets in the way. We are co-laborers together, not competitors in the ministry.

When we publicly value our volunteers and make sure a clean connection to ministry is established, we unleash the amazing power of creativity God built into them. It opens the door for our ministries to begin living the "infinitely more" dream God has for them. When that begins to happen, new ideas for ministry will inevitably rise to the surface. The smoldering ember of a new ministry idea can be ignited into a blaze of kingdom service when you champion the idea, give away control, and begin giving credit to others. When somebody has a good idea for a new ministry, tell them, "Great! You're it!" Challenge them to champion the idea and give them control over it. Then cheer for them as they go about making it happen. If you give someone a challenge, control, and credit, you're going to have a fulfilled, happy volunteer through whom God is doing things no one imagined were possible.

Be ambitious for your staff, for your volunteers, for other people—celebrate their contributions and go bonkers over their successes—don't be ambitious for yourself. If you can do this with sincerity, you will discover that obstacles you face in releasing your members will strangely disappear.

CHAPTER NINE

Connecting People and Needs

Encourage one another and build each other up, just as in fact you are doing. —1 Thessalonians 5:11 NIV

When I was an engineering student I heard an amazing story in one of my classes. It was back in the days of large computers—so large that they filled half a room and were programmed using card decks. Math was done on slide rules, calculators were just the four basic arithmetic functions, and laptop computers were science fiction.

One of the big aircraft manufacturing firms had been given the contract to develop a supersonic fighter jet to replace the aging aviation fleet currently in use. Computer modeling helped speed up the process tremendously, but there still remained the labor-intensive process of converting formulas to computer code and creating the card decks needed to program the computer to run the design simulations.

To speed up the process the engineers often shortened the calculations, leaving off constants or other terms in the equations that had little effect on the final result. It would be like our deciding to write a book using only three vowels and a dozen consonants rather than all twenty-six letters in the alphabet because it makes the process faster, thinking we could always add the rest of the letters back in when we have a final product. Evidently, this was a bad idea.

One of the designs made it to the prototype stage and an actual jet aircraft was built using the design. The test flights were incredible! Everyone was excited about this new aircraft until it started dropping out of the sky for apparently no reason. The plane would be flying along and then, at a particular altitude, airspeed, and angle of attack, simply lose lift and drop like a stone. Fortunately, control of the aircraft was easy to reacquire and the test flights were always at a safe altitude. No one was ever hurt, but more than a few had their heart rate checked!

A thorough investigation revealed a significant design flaw. Somewhere during the manufacture of the prototype, the performance requirements were changed slightly. No one thought to go back to the original design equations and make sure all the necessary data had been added back in based upon this recent design change. Consequently, the aircraft had to meet a flight performance need it had not been built to meet.

Matching people and needs in ministry is a lot like setting up that test flight. We hurry through the process and miss some small but key element, and the persons we recruit to do something crash on their first attempt to be successful—and since they are not professional test pilots, they go away discouraged. It usually happens something like this:

Common Leadership Wisdom: Use volunteers *wherever help is needed*—volunteers are a rare commodity!

The Tilt: Use volunteers *where they fit best*—mismatched volunteers burn out and bail out—that's one reason why they are a rare commodity!

A staff member pops her head into your office and says, "I need a volunteer who can work with Microsoft Excel." You say, "Great! I'll see who I can find!" You turn to your file, flip through a few index cards, and pull one out. This prospective volunteer indicated he knew Excel, so you shoot off an e-mail, asking him to get in touch with the staff member. You turn back to your desk with a smile. Another connection made, another volunteer released for kingdom ministry!

Except that when the volunteer shows up, your staff member says, "Please do this and that," and it turns out she needs someone who can create pivot tables. All that your volunteer knows how to do is input data and create simple formulas. The volunteer just sits and stares at the computer screen. He goes home discouraged, and now you have a staff member who is hot under the collar. "You sent me someone who didn't have a clue how to do what I needed," she says. "This is why I don't like using volunteers. It takes too much time, and I wind up doing it myself."

What can we do to avoid ugly scenes like this one? As people accept your invitation to serve, make sure they are connected properly. Everyone knows volunteers are essential to an effective ministry, and we certainly don't want to turn away people eager to serve. However, the tilt that makes a world of difference in nurturing your people and keeping them eager long-term is matching volunteers to opportunities and roles that truly suit their gifts and energies.

Pay attention to details and make sure the volunteer feels comfortable and capable. Mismatching a volunteer with a ministry opportunity does an injustice to both the ministry and the volunteer. Recruiting involves extending an invitation; it requires you to collect, categorize, and communicate. But once members have responded to the invitation, the paramount challenge is to effectively connect them into ministry by finding where their gifts best fit the needs of the ministry. If their first experience is a negative one, it will be four times as difficult to reengage them in the future.

It is important to realize that success is directly attributable to an intentional focus on fitting together what God is doing in the ministry and the attributes of the team called together to serve. Ask yourself if the various attributes of your team fit with God's goal for your ministry and capture your initial thoughts using the following table.

Category	Description	Does it fit?
Senior leader's statement of life purpose, personal vision, or mission		Yes/No
Ministry vision, aim, or purpose of the organization		Yes/No
Organizational needs regarding basic ministry functions		Yes/No
Target ministry needs of the community you serve		Yes/No
Where God is working in the ministry and in the community currently		Yes/No
The spiritual gifts, heart, abilities, personalities, and experiences of the ministry team		Yes/No

Excerpted from *Ministry Services: Team Design & Vocational Fit* © 2007 Jeffrey T. Jernigan. Used by permission.

No Minor Roles

In the life of a ministry, no roles are minor, no service small. Every task is important. Even the smallest detail, like sharpening pencils for the note takers, can make an eternal difference. Those little or "insignificant" chores no one wants to do may be far more important than anyone realizes at the time. The most discouraging thing in the world is doing a thankless task, week after week, without anyone noticing, much less pausing to express appreciation. Nothing sets people free in ministry like being affirmed and encouraged.

The Apostle Paul had been able to spend only a couple of weeks with the church in Thessalonica before he was forced by opposition to move on. Recognizing the need for church members to serve and appreciate one another in order for growth to occur, the letter he wrote to them is filled with good advice like this: "Encourage one another and build each other up, just as in fact you are doing" (1 Thessalonians 5:11 NIV). Those who serve are the heartbeat of a vibrant ministry. The ministry belongs to them, and apart from them the ministry can't become even a shadow of what God wants it to be. Ministry, however, is difficult. No matter how many exciting events are happening, servants can become discouraged—especially if their ministry is relatively uneventful. To be continually empowered, volunteers need to be affirmed and encouraged.

Research has shown that the sense of being validated can even increase one's self-esteem. For anyone working in ministry, being valued means feeling important, needed, developed, and appreciated—and it can make the difference between a ministry that is mobilized and one that is stagnant. We all want to make an eternal difference with our lives by serving beyond ourselves. We all need to be affirmed and to receive ministry ourselves.

Each of us can probably recall a time in ministry when we were not valued. We wondered if anyone cared at all about what we were doing. How did it make you feel? For someone who is pouring heart and soul into a ministry, being devalued is both humiliating and discouraging. As your staff and volunteers serve God, please commit to serving them with love, care, and—most important—with value! Make sure they know how much you value them.

Making a Clean Connection

Valuing your staff and volunteers, however, is a waste of time and effort (and may wind up hurting the hearts and ministries of staff members and volunteers) unless you strive to make a clean connection—a good match—between them and the challenges that they will face. No amount of affirmation will remove the pain of a mismatch between the need and their efforts that sends them plummeting to the ground because the lift under their wings suddenly disappeared.

Mastering "connection" is *the* most important skill you and your ministry can learn. Way too often ministry leaders say they've followed up, when what they meant was that they had e-mailed the person to ask if they "really" wanted to serve in their ministry. Once someone has taken on a challenge you asked them to, you need to get face-to-face with them and find out how it is going. Don't do your follow-up electronically. Here are four keys that have been proven to establish a clean connection between people and needs:

Key #1: Champion connection—If you use someone's time wisely, that person will give you more. Someone in your ministry has to monitor the quality of follow-up with people who have expressed an interest in ministry. The way to be sure people are getting cleanly connected into ministry is to empower someone on your team to champion the connection. Find a responsible person to champion ministrywide staff and volunteer appreciation to be certain that everyone is encouraged and affirmed in his or her service. Every ministry team should have a "volunteer connector." It's a simple name, but it defines the difference between a satisfied volunteer and a frustrated one. The volunteer connector's total goal is to value your volunteers.

Key #2: Connect immediately—When God speaks to persons about accepting an invitation to ministry and they respond, you have about seventy-two hours to get them connected before they start to second-guess the commitment they made. They start thinking about all the demands on their time and resources at work and at home and doubting whether they really can do what they have volunteered to do. You've got to get them connected immediately. To delay further is simply a lack of courtesy that people experience as disrespect. If you are not ready to hook them up with an opportunity, simply acknowledge their inquiry, let them know there is a delay, and tell them when you will get back to them. Silence is always understood negatively.

Cut the unnecessary steps out of the process people use to get connected. Get rid of the form that has to be filled out, collected, reviewed, passed on to the appropriate ministry leader, reviewed again, and then set up for a contact to be made. By then these good-hearted folks have moved on. Find a way to make that hard-copy or electronic indication of interest change hands only *once* before it ends up in the hands of an action-taker. Hey, don't say it's too hard! Hospitals do it all the time. They organize and connect *hundreds* of volunteers every week without a hitch. If you have run out of ideas, check with your local hospital, the Red Cross, or any other organization that depends exclusively on a volunteer workforce and ask them how they do it.

If you want people to get involved in ministry, it's best not to require them to jump through a bunch of hoops to get connected. Don't put an entire series of bureaucratic obstacles in their path. Connect them directly to the ministry, right where they are. If the invitation is extended in a meeting, Bible study, or small-group gathering, have a clipboard handy that can be passed around. Better yet, give them an e-mail or website address they can use to get hooked up immediately. If it is in a worship service, have a table set up nearby where they can go fill out a volunteer interest profile. The seventy-two-hour rule is simple—no response within seventy-two hours and you can probably kiss the volunteers goodbye.

Key #3: Capture key data—Obtain enough key information about each person to guarantee that he or she will be connected with the right ministry. You don't want to connect someone who is strongly introverted with the greeting team. Remember the S.H.A.P.E. paradigm and recognize that, even in—especially in!—volunteer positions, people perform best and are happiest doing what they love to do.

It is extremely important to quickly assess who these new volunteers are and capture that information so they can be connected with an appropriate ministry. New volunteers tend to think they don't have much time or much talent to offer. So we start by asking first-time volunteers three simple—yet strategic—questions:

1. *"How much time can you spend?"*—The first question new volunteers tend to ask is, "How much time will this take?" Most people today are strapped for time and want to maximize their minutes when serving God. This requires us to have a variety of opportunities, ranging in time requirement from less than one hour to more than ten hours. The goal is to ask how much time they have and then show them opportunities that align with their schedule.
2. *"What are your talents?"*—Knowing many people don't feel like they have much to offer the Lord, we want to help them see they can express their talents in simple ways that meet kingdom needs.
3. *"What team would you like to serve on?"*—Now we're getting closer to their heartbeat—revealing their passions. If they like serving youth, we connect them with the youth team's volunteer connector. If missions is on their heart, then we hook them up with the missions team volunteer connector.

Capturing this key data helps us make a clean connection. When we honor a person's time, talents, and passions, he or she feels empowered to fulfill his or her purpose.

Key #4: Contact them—Just as in communicating the available opportunities, personal connection is crucial when connecting a person to ministry. A letter or e-mail just won't do it. A phone call or, better yet, a face-to-face interaction is critical if the commitment of a new volunteer is going to be cemented firmly in place.

Most of us are reluctant to invest that level of effort. We've gotten in the habit of just dashing off an e-mail. Impersonal forms of communication may be simpler, but they are not effective enough. Require personal contact from staff members and ministry leaders. Go ahead and take the risk of having people think you're too demanding. It isn't trite to say that if Jesus valued a person enough to give his life for them, it's not too much for us to pick up the phone to call them.

When I was an executive in a mission organization as well as when I was a pastor in a traditional church setting, I kept an open-door policy. Staff and ministry leaders could come in at any time and count on my being available. It didn't matter what I was doing. There were no office hours or (unless I was on the phone or in a counseling session) closed-door rules. Yes, it meant a lot of interruptions and some days when my stuff didn't get done. But it also meant face-to-face resolution of innumerable issues, problems, questions, needs, and obstacles that otherwise would have interrupted ministry from the perspective of the experience of those we serve. Access and availability are the two greatest opportunities you as the team leader can provide that will enable the right connections at the right time for the right reasons.

Serving Central

Right about now, you may be thinking, *I understand these four keys and believe in them, but how can I make it happen?* We asked that question, too, and put together a team of experts to build an online tool designed to empower you and your ministry to "make the connection," bringing strengths and service together online. Check it out at www.servingcentral.com.

Serving Central is a fully customizable discovery and developmental system dedicated to helping you empower staff members, ministry leaders, and members to embrace their God-given strengths and express them in ministry and other life arenas. Serving Central has become the leading tool to match strengths and service together, helping many churches and ministries. It allows you to:

- Promote your ministries online. Members can use the Ministry Explorer feature to search for ministry opportunities, sign up, and start serving.
- Profile your members through the Serving Sweet Spot™ assessment. You will be able to see each person's strengths and use the Strengths Finder tool to sort through the various strengths within your church family.
- Place people by showing them the ministries that best match their strengths and passions. Once someone signs up, the appropriate ministry leader is notified via e-mail. The ministry leader can view the person's Serving Sweet Spot profile prior to contacting that person to help determine where that member might best fit within the ministry.
- Plot your progress through an array of online reports so you can see how many members are interested in serving, how many members have completed their Serving Sweet Spot assessment, how many members have been placed, and how many days it has been since a member expressed interest, yet is still without follow-up.

If you would like to check out Serving Central for a thirty-day trial period, please visit www.servingcentral.com and click on "30 day trial." If you decide to continue using Serving Central past the thirty days, your investment can be as low as one dollar a day.

What God Wants

Most ministries have more opportunities than people stepping up to fill them. The temptation in making a connection between the need and the people available to serve is to plug people in wherever the most compelling need exists. Sometimes this happens without regard to the people's gifts and skills or even their desires because the need is so great. In the long run this leaves damaged people and crippled ministries behind.

Perhaps one of the toughest disciplines to develop is the discipline of waiting—waiting until God raises up someone to stand in the gap. This kind of waiting is toughest on the leader because the leader must absorb the brunt of the criticism. Some will call you insensitive because they came to you with a great ministry idea, and when you encouraged them to take the leadership in getting this new idea off the ground, they balked and backed down. When you told them it wouldn't happen until God raised someone up to be the champion, they accused you of being parochial, uninterested in growing the ministry. But the truth is, unless God raises up someone who will lead this new effort from the perspective of a fresh calling, it isn't going to happen!

Sometimes you will have to say no to a good idea because it is inconsistent with your vision and the direction of the ministry. Every good thing to do is not always a necessary thing to do. If you are going to avoid being spread too thin with a diluted focus on what is important, you will have to say no to some great ideas. Others will not understand. Their passion is your distraction, and it will require extending grace on your part to help them through the disappointment of your refusal.

Some will want to reshape the vision. Vision is a peculiar thing. It starts out in your head but then ignites a fire in others who buy into it and own it as if it were their own. In some ways it is their own. A leader must balance the necessary and appropriate small shifts that occur in a vision because it is now corporate with the pressure from some to change the vision altogether. Incremental changes in the vision as you move forward in time are normal—as long as the core remains the same. Some adaptation to changing ministry realities is always needed. However, every once in a while you will run into someone who wants to hijack the vision and make it something different from what God has called you to do. Gently, in love, these people need to be encouraged to share their sunshine somewhere else if they cannot be true to the ministry God has called all of you to together.

When you intentionally form connections between people and needs, make sure that they all still point toward the same vision. Effort to effort, person to team, team to ministry, and ministry to vision—it should all link up in the same direction.

CHAPTER TEN

Value-Driven Behaviors

Be careful what you think, because your thoughts run your life.
—Proverbs 4:23 NCV

Consider a hospital in the 27th percentile in service. That means more than two-thirds of the rest of the hospitals in the country are better. Two years later the same hospital is winning awards. Four years later they are in the 99th percentile for some services and the 95th percentile for all other services. The turnaround makes the news.

Another example: Two years ago this manufacturing company was operating in a dilapidated, run-down factory in a seedy part of town. Now they are in a new factory, built from the ground up, that they moved into without missing a single day of production. In another year they double their revenue to $20 million, and they are in the news as well.

An international mission organization has to repatriate a third of their international staff and reinvent itself in an era when para-church organizations are having their identities challenged at every turn. But no one loses a job. No ministries are shut down in the affected countries. No one is fired. Instead, they intentionally shift their culture and come back stronger than ever.

A well-known denomination experiences a raft of pastors leaving the ministry. Fatigue has produced burnout and worse—moral failure. In a single year the trend is turned around.

A computer giant goes into the consulting business with a new twist, cultural planning, and becomes an international success. The Department of Social Services for the state incorporates the same cultural planning tools into its training for social workers.

A Christian humanitarian aid organization gains entrance into countries closed to every other Christian organization on the planet—bringing relief and the gospel to tens of thousands of people.

Two businessmen make possible an arrangement in which the former Soviet Union agrees with the Orthodox Church to no longer discriminate in the ranks based upon religion. That hits the news as well.

What do all these turnarounds have in common? They share a unique strategy, and the teams involved shared a commitment to invisibility, doing nothing to draw attention to themselves. In fact, they preferred invisibility as a practical application of being ambitious for the things of others and for what God was doing. Most important, they all shared a unique focus on value-driven behaviors. In other words, efforts were made to understand the organization's driving values and to operate out of that set. They understood what driving values were needed to turn things around and what needed to take place in order for that to happen.

One more thing they share: Gary.

Remember that shrinking church in the first chapter? Well, thanks to Gary, it has tripled in size. The church now has the reputation of being kingdom-minded, family-centered, and community-focused. This reputation is authenticated by folks coming to Christ left and right, volunteers stepping up out of nowhere, and the press in that city asking them for opinions on social issues! Ever heard of a dead church about to shut its doors being flipped in eighteen months? This one did it. Gary helped them.

Gary has also started two very successful companies in his career; worked in five different industries producing phenomenal turnarounds; and helped more churches, ministries, and Christian organizations than one would realize. He is driven by the values of integrity and humility and understands deeply that there is no limit to what you can accomplish if you are willing to let someone else take the credit. Gary is not unique. For every ministry guru, every luminary with a well-known name, you can count on *hundreds and thousands* of other men and women just like them who prefer success in anonymity.

> **Common Leadership Wisdom:** Equipping others for ministry begins with *answering the "how-to" questions.*
>
> **The Tilt:** Equipping others for ministry begins with *answering the "why" questions.*

These values are central to the ministry Gary has done. That is why it is important to understand Gary's story before we give you his tool. We do so love getting answers to the "how" questions, don't we? How-tos are important for cultivating our own leadership and for equipping others to lead. But it is the "why" that will revolutionize your ministry.

We are so pragmatic, so expert, so studied that at times it amazes me that we can do anything without the Holy Spirit. We've got all the "how-tos" down, but it is the Holy Spirit that gives us the motivation, the values—the "why"—to make a real difference. God must call, Jesus must send, and the Holy Spirit must energize your work or you will find yourself building nothing but an altar to your ego.

Obedience Is the Key

Gary found himself exhausted in a ministry that was going nowhere. Spiritual power was not evident and had not been for some time. It was as if God had abandoned the work. Much anguished prayer and introspection produced nothing. Where are you, God? Why isn't this ministry growing? What do you want me to do? You know the questions we ask in these times, and Gary was asking them all. God was not so much interested in Gary's doing, however, as he was in Gary's listening. "Samuel said, 'Has the Lord as great delight in burnt offerings and sacrifices, as in obeying the voice of the Lord? Behold, to obey is better than sacrifice, and to listen than the fat of rams'" (1 Samuel 15:22 ESV). This listening has a singular end in view—obedience.

The word *obedience* comes from the Latin word *audire*, which means "listening." On the other hand, the word *absurd* comes from the Latin word *surdus*, which means "deaf." When it comes to our calling to ministry, are we living an absurd life or an obedient life—deaf or listening to God? As Christians, too much of our understanding of obedience has been fashioned in negative ways by our culture. There is no negativity in God, and our obedience begins simply by listening positively. To do otherwise is absurd. Gary learned this lesson well not soon after his plea of desperation.

One day in church Gary was burdened by a comment from 2 Kings. In the following days it was pressed upon him continually to read this Old Testament book. So, Gary interrupted his devotional routine and began reading 2 Kings. When he got to chapter 5 his skin began to tingle. Naaman came to be healed of leprosy and a miracle occurred—spiritual power was not gone in Israel as some thought, but merely hidden from those without faith living in disobedience. The story of the floating axhead in chapter 6 reminded him that God can and does break out with power at times and in ways of his own choosing. When the King of Aram sends soldiers to kill Elisha and his servant is understandably inconsolable with fear, Elisha prays and suddenly there appears all around him the army of the Lord! They have never been alone. Eyes just needed to be opened.

Gary is overcome by a need to pray, but pray about what? In the middle of the night Gary is awakened with the single word *Haggai* ringing in his head. He asks, "Is that you, Lord? Do you want me to read Haggai? I haven't thought about that book in years; are you sure?" The word comes again, "Haggai." So Gary responds, "But I'm not done with Second Kings yet!" "Haggai" is the response. Gary caves in, "Okay, Lord, in the morning I will start reading Haggai."

Gary discovered over the next week as he read and prayed through this short little book that these people weren't listening to God. The key, he excitedly realized, was obedience! If we are not willing to listen to God about what needs to change, to have our eyes opened, so to speak, it will be human effort and not divine intervention behind our plans to turn things around. Real change occurs only at fundamental levels in the core of our being—our values. We can figure out how, but God has to get involved if we are going to truly understand the "why." That means we have to pray, listen, and be willing to respond in obedience no matter what the answer.

Gary discovered, for example, that the ministry team composed of paid staff and volunteers did not share in common the spiritual gifts related to evangelism or apostleship. No wonder their outreach efforts were failing! Most of the people working on the executive team were mavericks with little interest in pulling together. Getting them to commit to a common vision was like herding cats! Every goal, objective, and task must be matched with the appropriate values, practices, and attitudes if the ministry is to move forward with the least amount of friction in the inner workings as possible. These challenges were not a case of something wrong but a case of someone mismatched. As Gary and his team took into account each person's natural preferences, each person's God-given design, they could identify the value-driven behaviors represented in each person or team and match those to the results they needed in order to be successful.

Driving Values

Values mean different things to different people. For the sake of this discussion we are going to talk about a value as "a strong belief that thinking and acting in certain ways is going to produce the results you want or need." In other words, if I consistently behave in certain ways, I believe that I will have a good chance of obtaining an outcome that is important to me personally or socially—so important to me that I will consciously and unconsciously modify my behavior to ensure these outcomes. These behaviors reflect my driving values at any given time.

Each of us has six to eight driving values that are responsible for 90 percent of our behaviors *in the workplace* under normal conditions. This is an important distinction. Studies at Michigan State University, funded by the National Science Foundation, first explored the nature of human values in the 1970s and discovered that there is a set of values held by all people regardless of culture that influences their behavior in significant and predictable ways. In the 1980s this research was applied to the workplace and a set of driving values identified that proscribe our activities together whenever we agree together to accomplish something. In the 1990s these were applied to organizational development and eventually developed into a model for influencing change in people and groups.

If we know what workplace values best ensure the success of the organization's vision (broken down into goals, objectives, and tasks), and we know what spiritual gifts will best serve this vision, then we can build teams that have those values and gifts and use their natural preferences expressed as skills and talents to accomplish the vision in less time with less trouble. You know, it actually works! The problem is that it is too easy to leave out God. Without God it still may work—it just won't last.

Do you view proven tools as a means of manipulating people and circumstances or a means of removing obstacles to the entrance of the Holy Spirit into someone's life? If you opened the door for the Spirit of God, would he find you standing in the way? As consultants, coaches, and counselors, we have listened to thousands of ministry leaders in the last three decades. Do you know what the most prevalent limitation is that we face? Pride—

turned inward or outward. Insecure or arrogant, either one will eliminate success in ministry. Or, we can choose to be good stewards of what we know of human nature and use our knowledge to create a compelling and irresistible invitation for people to join us in the kingdom of God. After humiliating failures that exposed his bankruptcy, Gary chose to be kingdom-minded. Now he is a silent and largely invisible hero. If visibility is something you need, you need to be in theater, not ministry.

There are thirty-six values held in varying degrees by working people, whether the job is secular or ministerial in nature. Following is a list of these values and a thumbnail description of what they look like in action.

Knowledge	Spending time in the pursuit of knowledge, truth, and understanding
Help Society	Contributing to the betterment of the world or community I live in
Affiliation	Being part of a company, organization, or work team that accepts me as a team member
Stability	Having a work routine and job duties that are largely predictable and not likely to change over a period of time
Public Contact	Having a lot of day-to-day interaction with people
Physical Challenge	Facing physical demands that I find rewarding
Recognition	Earning rewards or public acknowledgment for the quality of my work

Leadership	Having the opportunity to lead others through direction, influence, and motivation
Security	Feeling assured of keeping my job and a reasonable financial reward
Artistic	Producing work with aesthetic value; engaging in creative work in any of several art forms
Creative Expressions	Expressing in writing or verbally my ideas, reactions, and observations
Job Tranquillity	Avoiding work-related pressures and the "rat race"
Moral Fulfillment	Feeling that my work is contributing to a set of moral standards that I feel are very important
Status	Having a position that others—my friends, family, and community—respect and value
Excitement	Experiencing a high degree of (or frequent) excitement in the course of my work
Power and Authority	Having the ability to control the work activities and rewards for others
Work Alone	Doing projects by myself, without any significant amount of contact with others
High Earnings	Anticipating financial rewards that will allow me to purchase those things I consider essential and the luxuries of the life I wish to live

Mental Stimulation	Constantly using my mind and continuing to develop my intellect
Fast Pace	Working rapidly and in an environment with a lot of activity
Responsibility	Making decisions and controlling my work domain; overseeing projects and/or personnel
Decision Making	Having the power to decide courses of action, policies, and so on
Change and Variety	Having responsibilities and activities that frequently change in their content and/or setting
Independence	Determining the nature of my work without significant direction from others; setting my own direction rather than merely following orders
Pressure	Working under time pressure and/or having the quality of my work judged critically by supervisors, customers, or others
Frontiers of Knowledge	Working in one of the physical sciences or human research; or working in a company that is technically excellent and striving for product advances
Influence	Changing others' attitudes or modifying their opinions, convincing them to do something or purchase something

Competition	Engaging in activities that pit my abilities against others' where there are clear win-and-lose outcomes
Time Freedom	Pursuing responsibilities according to my own schedule; no specific work hours required
Collegiality	Having close working relationships with a group; working as a team toward common goals
Competence	Working in those areas in which I feel I have talents and can excel
Leisure	Having enough time for leisure pursuits; no significant overtime required
Friendships	Developing close personal relationships with people as a result of my work activities
Challenge	Stretching myself with new, unique, or difficult issues to resolve
Precision	Working in situations in which there is little tolerance for error
Helping Others	Providing services or assistance to other people in a direct way, either individually or in small groups

For each of us, six to eight of these values are drivers at any given time in our lives. (See the appendix for an exercise you can use to determine your six to eight driving values.) They can change with our circumstances, but only slowly over time. If you could passively, by observation, assess the driving values in a ministry, or even better, assess them objectively by some survey methodology, and at the same time have an objective understanding of what driving values the vision required, you could come up with a gap analysis. You could know what the consensus of driving values was for any team or group or even organization and what was potentially needed. Now you have a target for change efforts, for team construction, even for hiring because you know what is missing. A real-life example may be helpful:

Let's say you are planning to take over the operation of a homeless shelter as part of your ministry. The previous Christian organization running the shelter has given their sixty-day notice to the city. There were problems with compliance to city regulations so now not only are you inheriting a ministry staffed with people you didn't choose, you have some peacemaking to do with city officials and the police department.

What values from the list above do you think would be key in moving forward with the team in place? Assume that after assessing the ministry, you came up with the following lists, comparing the ideal values for the new team and the values of the current team:

Ideal Team	Current Team
Help Society	Help Society
Stability	Status
Public Contact	Public Contact
Collegiality	Competition
Friendships	Leisure
Helping Others	Helping Others
Responsibility	Independence
Influence	Recognition

It is easy to see how if the current and ideal shared all values in common, they would potentially be well suited to serving the homeless and getting along well with the city officials and the police department. It is just as easy to see why the current team was having trouble doing this. The values of status, competition, leisure, independence, and recognition don't suit a team well that is supposed to be serving the community in a relatively thankless job that rarely gets recognition and is always underfunded. The challenge in this case is twofold: Influencing change in the consensus of values held by the team and ensuring new hires brought into the ministry contribute to the ideal value set.

When you add to this analysis of the values that drive a team's behavior an assessment of your passion, spiritual gifts, skills, and abilities from an organizational perspective, you have a human blueprint that will enable you to staff, structure, and send people out to do what they have been designed best to do by God! Now you are not only fitting people into their best roles, you are shaping the team and the organization.

CHAPTER ELEVEN

Influencing Change

Don't copy the behavior and customs of this world, but be a new and different person with a fresh newness in all you do and think. Then you will learn from your own experience how his ways will really satisfy you. —Romans 12:2 TLB

Leonard was so frustrated he could spit nails. This just shouldn't be! Everything had seemed so perfect when he began as the new senior pastor six months ago. Now the budget was a problem, despite the fact the church had more than five hundred in regular attendance. His staff of five was melting down and had moved in temperament from racehorses in harness to cats that needed to be herded. More volunteers than ever before were stepping forward but then just as quickly moving on when it seemed no one would really invest in them.

He was tempted to think it was he—the only new factor in the equation. But feedback had been strongly positive regarding his teaching and the elders consistently gave him high marks. What was going on? Why weren't things coming together? Leonard had been careful to involve stakeholders in the planning, communicate the new vision thoroughly and carefully over time, and win buy-in for the new directions the church was already moving toward when he came on board. Everything was in place: resources, people, vision, leadership—and it was all unraveling right before his eyes.

"The old has passed away; behold the new has come" we are reminded in 2 Corinthians 5:17 (ESV). Tucked in here is the idea that change as individuals or as a group is a process, not an event, a *transition* from the old to the new. This transition does not happen automatically but requires a stimulus, an influence that pervasively draws us into the new from the old based upon who we are *in Christ,* for it is only in Christ that we are changed and made new. This is a reference as well to our design and calling, our fit in the body of Christ, as it were. Here is what Leonard and his team discovered as they worked through this hiccup *together*.

Their strategic planning began well enough. Leonard pulled together the pastors, staff, elders, and ministry leaders in several sessions to work through their identity, internal strengths and weaknesses, external opportunities and problems, their assumptions about the ministry, a clear statement of mission and vision, and critical success factors. Over a number of meetings they worked out together goals, objectives, and tasks necessary to release people into an explosive ministry framed in a new vision everyone was excited about.

However, they did not consider very well *who* would be doing the work of this ministry and whether *together* they could support each goal with the driving values it would take to achieve them.

Strategic and Cultural Planning

140

They didn't consider the practices each underlying objective would require to be executed, or the specific behaviors each task would require for completion. This element really is cultural in nature since it incorporates how people working alone or in groups respond to their work environment and the expectations placed upon them in getting the work of the ministry done. Effective planning is both strategic with respect to goals, objectives, and tasks and cultural with respect to values, practices, and behaviors.

Change is inevitable in ministry, and any responsible leader will, of course, respond to changes with a plan for how to move forward in the new reality. This convention, however, sets us up to be reactionary, responding to changes in ministry only as they happen or after they occur. Communities grow and change, and the needs of those in our ministry shift as time goes by, life confronts us with new challenges that need to be responded to; the list could go on regarding all the different things that make constant change a reality for all of us in ministry. In part this is accommodated in our ministry budgets and plans. We anticipate as best we can what the future may hold and make our plans accordingly.

But this works only to a point. Our plans assume a certain degree of certainty in terms of the resources available to carry them out. What if the economy takes a turn for the worse and suddenly the resources are not there? How do you shift your plans, make large-scale changes, when that possibility is on the horizon? What if your plan requires certain attitudes and values your team doesn't possess? How do you build those things into them? What perspectives or convictions are needed ministrywide for the success of your vision? How do you influence a change in these things if they are not already present in your people?

Inevitably when we do not

Common Leadership Wisdom: As time goes on change is inevitable in ministry and should be responded to with good planning.

The Tilt: It is important to manage change rather than allowing change to manage the ministry.

take these things into account we end up allowing change to manage us. Ministries that don't operate based on sound planning experience this even more than ministries that do plan. There is a way to stay out in front, anticipating the need for change and influencing its direction and outcome. Strategic and cultural planning is all about the things that have to be accomplished as well as the people who must accomplish them. We can have perfect plans and unlimited resources and still fail if we haven't incorporated planning around the people factor as well.

Influencing Change in Values

When Leonard and his team began the process of executing their plan, they immediately ran into some key mismatches between people and projects. Now, trying to make everything fit perfectly into some giant ministry machine can be carried to the extreme. That is definitely not where this is going. However, there are some key alignments that do warrant attention in the larger view of planning.

We helped Leonard back up and put the cultural planning piece in place, and we made some interesting discoveries. As in the example of the homeless shelter we presented in chapter 10, the driving values shared by the team members were very different from the set of values the team would ideally share in order to complete the tasks, accomplish the objectives, and fulfill the goals.

Team's Actual Values	Team's Ideal Values
Power and Authority	Exercise Competence
Friendships	Public Contact
Exercise Competence	Moral Fulfillment
Stability	Friendships
Knowledge	Fast Pace

Job Tranquillity	Responsibility
Helping Others	Helping Others
Status	Change and Variety

Only three values—Friendships, Exercise Competence, and Helping Others—are shared in common by both lists. Now, you don't have to have identical lists to succeed in your plans, but you do need more than just three out of eight. In fact, some of the values held by the team will actually work against the success of the plan. Valuing Power and Authority aim to control the work activities and rewards for others and will work against Responsibility, the opportunity for decision making and control over one's work domain; the chance to oversee projects and/or personnel. It is the old tension between autocratic, centralized control and pushing freedom to act down to the level where people affected by the decisions can make them together. Stability looks for a work routine and job duties that are largely predictable and not likely to change over a long period of time, while Change and Variety focus on work responsibilities and activities, which frequently change in their content and/or setting. The plan calls for a flexibility the team doesn't yet have.

It is not realistic to expect everyone on the team to share the same driving values. What is important to understand is which driving values they do share in common to some degree and how that consensus compares to the driving values the work will actually require. It is no wonder the team was reacting independently, like cats that needed herding! Their driving values were taking them in different directions. This is really an opportunity to *influence change* in your team members' driving values.

These values change all the time in response to the leadership provided and the environment created in which the plan is to be carried out. We are motivated by, or we put energy into, those things we believe are needs that must be met, whether those needs are personal or more altruistically needs of the ministry. So, how do we reframe the need? How do we create alignment on the team around the same things? How do we get people to value enough of the same things that there is real teamwork releasing real power in the ministry?

Influencing Change in Fit

The next thing we discovered was that a number of the team members were mismatched to the work that needed to be done. All of us have natural preferences, ways of thinking and acting in the workplace that are more normal than other ways. It is our S.H.A.P.E. working itself out in patterned ways—how we communicate, what kind of work we do best, the pace and level of challenge that stimulates us more than it fatigues us. No one works in a groove like this all the time—but we do want people working at things they enjoy doing more than things they dislike doing, things that are a constant struggle, or things that frustrate them, even though we all from time to time do things we dislike, that are a struggle, and leave us frustrated.

Patterned behaviors in the workplace produce practices commonly used to get things done. They may be written down and take the form of policies or procedures, or they may be more informal, a reflection of unofficial guidelines and "how we do things around here." If we fit people to the work that needs to be done at least marginally well, healthy patterns and practices will emerge. Let's say it this way: Patterned behaviors produce practices. If we know what behaviors (related to skills, attitudes, experiences, and passion) the tasks will require, and we know what ways of getting things done (practices) are needed, then we have a means of creating alignment between our goals, objectives, and tasks and our values, practices, and behaviors.

Then there is the matter of spiritual gifts. Leonard's vision included reaching a large Spanish-speaking neighborhood near the church. They had a Spanish-speaking pastor lined up, added another service into the schedule, and put a team together. However, none of them had the gift of evangelism or anything close to an apostolic gifting. Their hospitality ministry was missing—yes, you guessed correctly—anyone with the gift of hospitality! The counseling ministry was loaded with teachers—none with discernment, mercy, or helps in their gift mix. Many of these great people were frustrated in their efforts until they were provided some basic teaching on spiritual gifts and given the opportunity to identify their gift mix and how and where it could best be applied.

Creating alignment in the ministry doesn't have to be complicated. Assume for a moment that your team goal is to climb Mount Everest. A reasonable objective would be to train and prepare for achieving this goal. Lots of tasks come to mind. Someone needs to create a physical conditioning regimen. Someone else needs to select and purchase the right clothing and equipment to use. Someone needs to scout out practice areas to use in advance of the real thing. Someone needs to spend hours on the phone setting up all the transportation and lodging. You get the idea. Lots of very different tasks are involved.

Now imagine a team that has taken on these tasks based on their unique design and calling. Imagine them developing the patterns and then the practices that will get them through the three-year process of preparing for and then succeeding in achieving the objective. Imagine them all pulling together with the same mind and the same values, climbing that mountain, and fulfilling the goal. Sure, there are obstacles along the way and things go wrong. But by and large—imagine it—your team did it all with unusual commitment, energy, and excitement; better than any other team on the mountain.

Your vision for ministry is the mountain you need to conquer. This approach of considering the values involved; the skills, talents, and experience needed; the spiritual gifting that will bring real power to the ministry, may seem like just another method, no better or worse than other methods you have been exposed to. In the previous chapter, we defined a value as a strong belief that thinking and acting in certain ways is going to produce the results you want or need.

This idea actually comes out of Scripture. Think about Ezra, Nehemiah, Haggai, and Zechariah—all prophets focused on rebuilding not just the temple and the city walls, but religious life in Israel. Take some time to read their books, looking for what they strongly believed about the way people needed to think and act during this time of transition and transformation. Watch how they match people up with what they do best with sensitivity to God's calling and design in each. Perhaps the best example of driving values from this perspective can be found in Jesus' words in the Sermon on the Mount. Paul is also very clear about the role of skills, talents, gifts, and passion in his discussion of these things in his letters to the Romans, Corinthians, and Ephesians.

So, back to the present—how do we influence change in people and groups so this kind of empowerment in ministry actually takes place? The same things that Ezra, Nehemiah, Haggai, and Zechariah needed; Jesus modeled; and Paul taught: a plan, the right kind of leadership, the right kind of environment, and the intervention of almighty God!

Have a Plan

Some people prefer not to plan but like instead to go with the flow. Unfortunately, going with the flow can take you off in the wrong direction or in no direction at all. Surely the Spirit will still move even without our help, but here's the tilt: Even God has a plan. " 'Woe to the rebellious children,' declares the LORD, 'who execute a plan, but not *Mine*' " (Isaiah 30:1 NASB, emphasis added). Then bathe your plans in prayer that they might reflect the mind of God. Ultimately, if our plan is not his plan, we are planning to fail. The creation story alone should be enough to remind us that God thinks things through, is organized, has a sense of priority, and plans. We are all made in his image.

Planning can be as simple as some notes on a napkin or the result of a team-based process over a number of days. It really depends upon what you are planning to do—how large or small, how simple or complex, how labor-intensive or system-dependent. The bottom line is: Have a plan. It seems so obvious to say we have to make sure our plans are really a reflection of God's. Yet when we work with ministry leaders all over the world and ask the question, "What is your plan?" you would be amazed at some of the answers we get:

"Oh, I don't have a plan. I just follow where the Spirit leads."

"My plan is in my head and I follow it, mostly; sometimes not."

"I wrote my plan down but don't show it to anyone because they want to make changes to it."

"Yeah, we did strategic planning. But then it just sat in a drawer until it was time to plan again."

"We just plan from project to project and campaign to campaign. It's a lot easier that way."

All these people are planning to fail to some degree. Have a plan. Take into consideration the things that need to be done and the kinds of people you will need to do them and what will be required to fit them into your mountain-conquering team. Use your plan. Revisit the plan often with your team and make adjustments. If God is not bringing along the right people with the right stuff, don't settle for less and plug someone into the hole on your team. Be willing to let things go undone until God raises up the right person with the right gifts and passion.

Provide the Right Kind of Leadership

Leadership in change is unlike any other kind of leadership, and it goes far beyond mere authority. Authority refers to the legitimacy or justification to exercise power. Power is the ability to achieve certain ends. Authority doesn't make you a leader, it simply gives you power. Leadership is influencing others to act. That influence may be exercised through a number of different styles of leadership including autocratic, bureaucratic, charismatic, relational, participative, and transactional, just to name a few. Each of us has a natural or preferred style of leadership. In addition, we must master other styles as well because in change different people and groups in different and varying situations will require *different* leadership styles in order to be effective.

Those of us who can exercise authority in only a limited range of styles will sooner or later run into circumstances in which we are powerless to influence change and growth. In those situations we must pass the mantle to someone else (who may still report to us) who has the best style for unleashing the power in people to get things done. Leonard was an autocratic leader. He was not comfortable with other styles. But some aspects of the vision, and the plan created to support it, required participative leadership to pull off—it was going to take a team of interdependent people. Volunteers, for example, need the more people-centered influence of relational leadership in recruiting and more transactional leadership later on in being directed and sustained in the work they have volunteered to do.

An administrative pastor better have a bent for bureaucratic leadership in his or her repertoire if the pastor is going to handle operations and finance well—which brings up another thought about leadership in change. Don't depend on policies, procedures, rules, guidelines, reporting relationships, and such to get things done. It is easy to make the mistake of depending upon these things to leverage behaviors. Organizational structure, policies, and rules don't produce results—they organize the work so that people can produce the results.

In times of transition, which is what implementing your vision in ministry will create, the leadership we exercise must acknowledge that we are all spiritual beings having a human experience and not human beings having a spiritual experience. If you are doing the work that God approves, it will *always* require transition, change, and spiritual transformation! Transformation is a spiritual process that transcends our humanity. Human ingenuity, knowledge, and expertise will not be enough to create lasting change at fundamental levels. Our leadership must be *spiritual* in nature:

> When I came to you, brethren, I did not come with superiority of speech or of wisdom, proclaiming to you the testimony of God. For I determined to know nothing among you except Jesus Christ, and Him crucified. And I was with you in weakness and in fear and in much trembling, and my message and my preaching were not in persuasive words of wisdom, but in demonstration of the Spirit and of power, so that your faith would not rest on the wisdom of men, but on the power of God. (1 Corinthians 2:1-5 NASB)

This means that we must look to the word for our understanding of what spiritual versus human leadership looks like:

> Jesus called them to him and said, "You know that the rulers of the Gentiles lord it over them, and their great ones exercise authority over them. It shall not be so among you. But whoever would be great among you must be your servant, and whoever would be first among you must be your slave, even as the Son of Man came not to be served but to serve,

and to give his life as a ransom for many." (Matthew 20:25-28 ESV)

We are called to be servants. Our job is to make others successful, not insist that they make us successful.

Create the Right Environment

What can we do to create a climate conducive to those in our ministries voluntarily choosing to align their goals, expectations, and desires with those of the ministry? How does the vision so capture them that they adopt as their needs the needs of the ministry? Creating this kind of alignment is the secret to unlocking and releasing the team's motivation.

If Leonard's organization were an international company employing thousands, we would approach the issue of organizational change differently. *Management by Value*© incorporates eight steps in influencing change in people and groups when the delivery of a product or service is the goal. But Leonard's organization is not a business, it is a ministry, and the ministry goals all have to do with caring for people in one way or another. That makes it very simple. Teaching people how to care for people is fundamentally a matter of modeling: "You have heard me teach things that have been confirmed by many reliable witnesses. Now teach these truths to other trustworthy people who will be able to pass them on to others" (2 Timothy 2:2 NLT). Other translations use words like *commit* and *entrust* in describing Paul's influence in reproducing himself in others.

It is clear from Paul's life that modeling took many forms. One of these we would describe as creating informal learning environments. Paul was in the word and prayer often with his team. Modeling this, Leonard began his weekly staff meetings with an *hour* in Bible study and prayer before getting on to the business at hand. The emphasis of each study had something to do with change and the values the team needed to adopt. Prayer focused on the challenges they faced in moving ahead and waiting on the Lord's timing to make moves. Leonard began as well to practice in his own lifestyle the values central to the team's success. God's design and calling, each person's unique sphere of ministry, and the central theme of the vision became the silver thread running through every communication, every meeting, and every personal appointment with his staff.

Leonard began to understand experientially how most things in ministry are caught, not taught. In other words, something lived out and practiced creates more readiness learning moments than a lesson laid out classroom-style. Leonard also began to emphasize relational competence over technical competence. Success of the vision would depend upon people, not programs, and that meant equipping people to deal with conflict, misunderstanding, discouragement, failure, and all of the trip, stumble, and fall kinds of things that attend change processes.

Over the first twelve weeks or so of backing up and starting over with the execution of the plan, Leonard learned a few things about himself as well. He discovered he was overly sensitive to criticism and would often rush to defend himself. It was easy sometimes to make excuses for the failures and look in his heart for someone or some circumstance to blame. He recognized how his intolerance and inflexibility stifled and held back some of the creative people on the team in unproductive ways. Leonard also found out that he was a micromanager.

Micromanagement kills spiritual transformation in ministries because it robs the team of the benefit of their collective input and it substitutes human influence and direction for the Holy Spirit's influence and direction. Here are some characteristics of micromanagement as contrasted with an ideal environment:

	Micromanaged Environment	*Ideal Environment*
Authority	Favors close control, central authority, and limited decision making for employees, rigid.	Favors empowering employees, makes positive assumptions about human nature, flexible.
Orientation	Primarily technical, specialists.	Primarily business, generalists.
Control	Compliance control: Employees cannot or will not make responsible and competent choices about their behavior and performance at work. Task requirements must be proscribed in detail, checked regularly, and variance penalized. Control people.	Commitment control: Appropriate training, education, information, systems, and support will enable employees to make choices and decisions that will allow the company to focus resources effectively. Control processes.
Temperament	Build: Change is suspect, literal, detail-oriented, logical, high need for closure, cautious.	Create: Change is necessary, intuitive, pattern- or trend-oriented, logical, risk taker, high need for freedom.
Focus	Naturally tactical, prefers structure, unimaginative, secretive, tense, likes consistency, perfectionist, anxious at times.	Naturally strategic, prefers freedom to act, imaginative, reflective, likes variety, intense, quick.

Structure	Overstructures to provide safety and security, constant sense of dissatisfaction, hierarchical, assigns responsibility, avoids confrontation.	Coach, mentor, leads by questions, minimizes structure, constant sense of movement, delegates authority, uses confrontation.
Leadership	Defer to rules for control, insistent, policy-based, autocratic.	Use rules to guide and direct, models, principle-based, participative.

Through the Looking Glass: A Practical Guide to Strategic and Cultural Change, Jernigan, HVG, 2000.

In order to effectively lead his team through this period of transformation in the ministry, Leonard was going to have to reexamine his thinking about spiritual leadership. Micromanagers usually subscribe to most of the following foundational beliefs:

Micromanaged Environment	*Ideal Environment*
People are naturally lazy; they prefer to be told what to do and led on a leash.	People are naturally active; they set goals and enjoy striving.
People work mostly for money and status awards.	People seek many satisfactions in work beyond just money and status.
The main focus that keeps people productive at work is their fear of demotion or termination.	The main force keeping people productive at work is their personal and social goals.

People are children grown larger; they are naturally dependent on leaders.	People normally mature beyond childhood; they aspire to independence, self-fulfillment, and responsibility.
People expect and depend on direction from above; they do not want to think for themselves.	People close to the situation see and feel what is needed and are capable of self-direction.
People need to be told, shown, and trained in proper methods of work.	People who understand and care about what they are doing can devise and improve their own methods of doing work.
People need supervisors who will watch them closely enough to be able to praise good work and reprimand errors.	People need a sense that they are respected as capable of assuming responsibility and self-correction.
People have little concern beyond their immediate material needs.	People seek to give meaning to their lives by identifying with various entities including companies.
People need specific instruction on what to do and how to do it; larger policy issues are none of their business.	People need ever-increasing understanding; they need to grasp the meaning of the activities in which they are engaged.
People appreciate being treated with courtesy.	People crave genuine respect from others.
People are naturally compartmentalized.	People are naturally integrated.
People naturally resist change because they prefer old ways.	People tire of monotony, enjoy new experiences, are creative to some degree, and resist change out of habit.

Jobs are primary and people are selected, trained, and fitted to predefined jobs.	People constantly grow and seek self-realization; jobs must be designed, modified, and fitted to people.
People are what they are and remain static as adults.	People continue to learn and grow as adults.
People need to be inspired or pushed down or driven.	People need to be released and encouraged and assisted.

Through the Looking Glass: A Practical Guide to Strategic and Cultural Change, Jernigan, HVG, 2000.

From *Tilt: Small Shifts in Leadership That Make a Big Difference* © 2010 by Erik Rees and Jeff Jernigan. Used by permission.

You establish the climate in your organization. Things like sensitivity to criticism, defensiveness, fear of failure, blame shifting, inflexibility, and micromanagement must go. The best leaders in change are fallible leaders who know how to create an environment in which experimentation and failure are okay to a point, where sometimes the best answers are just guesses, and mistakes aren't cause for crucifixion.

Cry Out to God

In seminary I met a man who grew up and came to Christ in Communist China. His testimony was incredible, but that is not what I remember him for best. Just before graduating and getting ready to return to China, he was asked what his impressions were of American Christians. Among the many favorable things he noted was an incredible observation.

"America," he said, "has so many resources at its disposal and has the benefit of such excellent educational opportunities that we can do just about anything we set our minds to. It is amazing, in light of this, how much the church in America can get done without the Holy Spirit!" Now that remark stuck with me!

We do have some great tools at our disposal and some great thinking about how to use them. We could just forge ahead with making a difference and assume because things change that God was in it. But, oh how glorious would the change have been if indeed we had cried out to God to fill us with his Spirit for every good work! Instead, we often don't know what we are missing. All the change agents we find in the Bible, including Jesus, cried out to God for his help, his wisdom, and his will and not their own.

"In the day of my trouble I will call to you, for you will answer me" (Psalm 86:7 NIV). The psalmist describes his confidence in God as a ready answer to his call, and the idea here is that he cries aloud with the expectation he will be heard. I can just picture them doing this: "Hey, God! I am in trouble here! What do you have for me in this situation?"

Sometimes I want to whisper my cries for help as if someone might overhear me and be disturbed. But this really isn't what God is interested in. Jesus Christ has purchased for us bold access to the throne! Isaiah tells us to lift up our voice with a shout and not be afraid of being overheard (Isaiah 40:9).

If I want bold answers, I am going to ask for them boldly! Then I can say with David, "I love the LORD, for he heard my voice; he heard my cry for mercy" (Psalm 116:1 NIV). Practice your boldness! Ask God for answers and don't be timid about it! It doesn't matter if your prayer is voiced out loud or in the silent cry of your heart. God isn't hard of hearing and hears even a groan without words. His ears don't miss a single sigh that escapes our lips. He loves to answer our prayers and wants us to be intentional in seeking him out so that he can be intentional in responding to us. Take time to pray. Life will be forever changed for you and those you seek to influence.

PART III

SUSTAINING YOUR LEADERSHIP

CHAPTER TWELVE

Leading from the Tilt

It is God himself who has made us what we are and given us new lives from Christ Jesus; and long ages ago he planned that we should spend these lives in helping others. —Ephesians 2:10 TLB

One day in Roswell, New Mexico, God changed my life. It didn't involve a UFO, either. Rather, God used an amazing small group at Grace Community Church to make it happen.

I was there to lead an "Only You Can Be You" conference for the church. After the first session, Lendell Nolan, the congregation's pastor of ministries, said to me, "I want you to meet this small group that I led through the S.H.A.P.E. study" (a study I created to help people discover their God-given design and purpose).

As we stepped out into the hallway, I fully expected to meet several young adults, chat for a few minutes, and get back to the conference. Instead, the group that greeted me— while they were young adults—turned out to be, each one, an individual with a disability. Each one lived every day with incredible life challenges, yet in that moment I was the one who was speechless. We have a lot of special-needs people in our church, but I have to confess before God that I had never before even thought about them and the role they ought to play as ministers in the church. They were not on my radar whatsoever, and I'd never before seen them represented as a small group in this way. Lendell had incorporated a number of the tilts we've discussed in this book into his ministry, and one of the evidences of what a difference small shifts toward empowering leadership can make was there before my eyes—an incredible group of enthusiastic, energized, and committed people released to do what God designed into every cell in their body—and with more joy than I had seen in teams not challenged in life by limitations as these folks were!

One of the young men in the group quoted what to me was a familiar line: "I'm a masterpiece," he said, his voice ringing with conviction. It was a quote from my book *S.H.A.P.E.: Finding and Fulfilling Your Unique Purpose for Life*. In that moment, my life changed forever.

Now some people would look at a person who struggles to walk or talk and say, "A masterpiece? You've got to be kidding." Some people even turn their backs on these individuals, or look the other way. But if God has placed a special-needs person in your church, you've got to know that person isn't there by accident. In just the same way that God made you as a masterpiece of his creation, so he made them to reflect his beauty. These special people have a role to play in the church that no one else can fulfill. And we in church leadership need to figure out how to tap into their uniqueness.

Wondering, I thought about the many hundreds, even thousands of people we have helped along the road to spiritual maturity who somehow missed the tilt and are just doing "okay" these days but not really soaring. Why are they any different from these people? Then it hit me. These wonderful people had been forced by their disabilities to look inward in identifying who they were in the unencumbered total freedom of the soul. In understanding the masterpiece they found within, because of their very real limitations, they were forced to tilt their perspective on life and ministry, and that made the difference for them. They had to look at doing the same old things in brand-new ways because the old ways were not available to them. Looking at old things in new ways and finding answers—now that is what the tilt is all about, and it is a way of life for special-needs persons.

Years ago, I met a fellow who was assistant director of the student ministry at the major university in the southwest. Affected by cerebral palsy since birth, he walked and talked only with great difficulty. But he served full-time as a volunteer among the university's 400 students with disabilities—the largest concentration of such students in the world at the time.

Besides counseling these students with disabilities, he also equipped other Baptist students to meet the needs of the physically disabled people in their midst and taught church groups how to minister to the disabled and their families. What better person could God have tapped for that ministry?

This truly gifted gentleman once said: "It takes a mature person to see the inside of someone before the outside. But as important as it is to know a person's needs, it's more important to know their strengths. People rarely stop to ask what a physically disabled person can contribute. Only God can turn an affliction into a gift."

That young man was right. God absolutely created him to be a masterpiece, just as he has made you and everyone else in your church to be a reflection of his handiwork. Most of us start out looking at those on our team, volunteers stepping up for the first time, and even the folks in our ministries with a "show me" attitude. Show me what you can do, prove to me you have what it takes, demonstrate first that you are a masterpiece, and then we can talk about your role in ministry. Leading from the tilt means assuming those serving with us, those wanting to serve, and those whom we serve are all masterpieces to begin with. All we can do is invest in them further, helping them discover God's art in their lives. But to do that we need to master the art and science of the tilt ourselves, learning to recognize those subtle shifts that will take us to new heights.

Laying a Foundation

Leading from the tilt involves investing in masterpieces to continually hone what God has made, enabling people to live up to that God-shaped potential in each of their lives. So often in ministry we simply place people in roles where they can be of some service, and that is the end of the story. What a wonderful testimony it would be if, when God moves them on to other opportunities in other ministries, they could say of their time with us, "I am a better person because of my time there. I really grew. They helped me develop into my potential."

As you invite people to serve and release them into ministry, you have a responsibility to invest in them and help them develop their God-given strengths. If everyone in your ministry is going to hear and respond to God's call, the entire body must be built on a solid foundation. They must hear and understand that God's plan is for each member to be a minister on mission. Each person needs to recognize that God has uniquely designed him or her for a specific ministry only he or she can accomplish. You can cultivate an empowering ministry by investing in the life of each person, reinforcing the "every member a minister on mission" message in every aspect of life.

There are dozens of ways to accomplish this goal. The key is to have a balanced plan that will give you the highest return on investment for God. A solid investment plan should include many options so people can learn how God has designed them through all the different learning styles. Many lessons will be learned the hard way. Here are a few key lessons we've learned through trial and error:

When it comes to developing new ministries, time is on your side. It is prudent to not rush the process. If an idea is truly from God, it will stand the test of time. God will provide the resources at the times he knows they are needed. Many potential new ministry leaders want to hurry through the process. Experience has shown us that those leaders who are in the greatest hurry often are not attuned to God's voice.

A servant heart is required for ministry leadership. A potential new leader ought to demonstrate a spirit of cooperation and a desire to put the good of others and the welfare of the congregation above his or her own interests. A lack of cooperation with leadership and the established process of new ministry development may indicate a future problem and should raise red flags.

In all matters regarding this ministry, prayer warriors are needed. Far too often, new ministry ideas are launched into the life of the church without adequate prayer preparation. Each and every decision must involve the Lord. Making decisions on our own, without seeking specific direction from God, leaves us open to the possibility that we might start something he will not bless.

You must be willing to ask tough questions. "Will you gain financially at all from this ministry?" Sometimes people use ministry ideas as ways to promote their vocation. "Will your family support you in this ministry?" Sometimes people use ministry to get out of a painful situation in their home. "Should this new ministry just be added to an existing one?" Sometimes a new idea becomes a new program in an existing ministry.

Fostering New Ministry Dreams

One of the biggest challenges to becoming an empowering leader is giving up control, setting others free to succeed—or to fail. One reason many ministries don't experience the excitement of empowering ministry is that they are structured for control, rather than for growth. You can tell whether a ministry is focused on control or on growth by the reception persons get when they approach a staff member with an idea for a new ministry. Are they discouraged or embraced? Do we say "Oh, no" or "Oh, great"? Do we come up with a dozen reasons why their idea won't work? Or do we launch them into a process to discover God's plan for their ministry idea?

The Bible teaches that the members are the real ministers, which means members will have new ministry ideas. Not every idea, however, ought to become reality. God expects excellence in ministry, so before new ministry ideas are launched into the life of the church, they should meet certain basic qualifications. Once that hurdle has been passed, a plan must be developed to ensure the new ministry will enhance the church's vision and mission.

Here are seven suggested qualifications every new ministry should meet before it is launched:

1. **The ministry idea must be biblically sound.** Someone in our church once suggested that everybody in our congregation who traveled should grab a couple of extra soaps and shampoos from the carts that are always in the hallways of hotels. If everyone who traveled brought those items back to the church, they could be given to the homeless. While the intent may have been right, stealing soap and shampoo from the hotel is not biblically sound, no matter who is helped in the process. Obedience to God should always come first.

2. **The idea should build the reputation of the ministry in the community.** If people discovered our church was swiping the soap and shampoo we used in homeless ministry, the reputation of the congregation would be damaged far beyond any good we were doing for the community.

3. **The new idea represents a primary motive to serve.** A leader is responsible to identify the motives of people who want to start new ministries. Let's say, for example, that you have a member who wants to start a ministry advising people on money management. You have to ask this member a tough question: "Will you benefit financially in any way from this ministry?" Consciously or unconsciously, members often suggest ministries that will benefit them financially or in some other self-serving way. A ministry motivated by selfish ambition ought to make us uncomfortable enough to say no to this idea.

4. **The idea must fulfill one or more of the purposes, goals, or priorities found in the strategic and cultural plan.** We firmly believe that God created the church to fulfill five purposes: fellowship, discipleship, worship, ministry, and evangelism. We believe that God blesses the ministry that balances its focus on all five of the purposes—and that activities that do not fulfill the purposes are a distraction from our mission in the world. If a new ministry idea cannot be shown to fulfill at least one of the purposes, we don't launch it. Both of us serve on pastoral staff in purpose-driven ministries in very different faith traditions. The model for being purpose-driven finds its roots in Scripture and not in any particular spokesperson or denominational tradition. More important, it works! Hence, our strong feelings on this one.

5. **The ministry idea must be transferable to other ministries.** Use transferable concepts whenever you can. Ideas that can work across social and cultural boundaries will be useful in ministries around the world. Pray that what you develop will be useful to other churches and ministries, regardless of their size. When new ministry ideas are suggested, ask, "Will this idea work in both Nebraska and Nigeria?" If it won't, don't use it.

6. **The ministry idea must be led by a team.** Someone may come to us, saying, "I have this vision from the Lord. I want to start this ministry, and it needs to be started this week." We want to be sure the potential new leader is attuned to God's voice. For that reason, we won't agree to launch a ministry until a team of four people is in place to launch it so the ministry isn't interrupted if a leader has to withdraw.

7. **The leadership team members must demonstrate spiritual maturity.** No, they don't have to be spiritual giants! We simply want our ministry leaders to be solidly grounded. That requires at least a minimal foundation in membership, maturity, ministry, and mission.

Developing Emerging Leadership

Today at lunch, three of us, all pastors, were talking about our most memorable moments. We have more than seventy-five years of combined experience as pastors and missionaries, and two of us have more than fifty years of combined experience in the corporate world and as business owners. You would think the stories would be legend! The youngest one among us, however, shut the discussion down with his most memorable moment.

He looked across the table when it was his turn and said to Bud, "My most memorable moment was just a few weeks ago when I looked at some of my archived teachings on the church's website. Do you know what I saw? I saw you." Bud sat there with puzzlement flickering across his face.

"I saw you teaching me more than twenty years ago. I saw your mannerisms, heard your expressions, and felt your humor in my laugh! You were and still are my hero, my mentor." But even that was not what caught my attention.

"You know, there is a lot of talk these days about the emerging church, reproducible concepts, sustainable ministry, readiness learning moments; and I suppose those skills are important. But what I learned from you is that Jesus died for people, not for methods. Jesus loved people, not buildings. Jesus transformed lives and not ministries. What I learned from you is that the mission is people."

My heart nearly stopped. You see, I know that this pastor is a friend and mentor of sorts to my coauthor, and I see the same heartbeat, *the same tilt,* in him. Three generations marching to the beat of the same drum. One that the Apostle Paul identified in 2 Timothy 2:2: What you want to pass on to others you need to live out in front of them.

So, how do you teach and model what it means to make people the vision and mission while at the same time trying to be organized, disciplined, and effective in ministry? Well, here are

166

four tactics, organized by the acronym T.E.A.M., that will help put the emphasis on the right thing in developing emerging leadership on your team.

Common Leadership Wisdom: *Keeping people's focus* on the vision and mission are the most important things a leader can do.

The Tilt: People *are* the vision and mission.

Train—Sharpening the Ministry

Someone needs to focus on the service of the ministry. The challenge of the Training Coach is to strengthen the commitment of the members to service. The Training Coach believes an effective ministry provides quality service through excellent training. The reason for this role is to strengthen the ministry by developing the skill level of those involved in the ministry. This element of leadership provides members with the opportunity to improve their ability to express their God-given strengths in service.

Encourage—Shepherding the Ministry

Someone needs to focus on the shepherding care and development of small groups within the ministry. The challenge of the Shepherd Coach is to strengthen the commitment of the members to one another. The Shepherd Coach believes an effective ministry flows out of the abundant life of its members. The reason for this role is to ensure every member is connected and cared for within the ministry. This element of leadership provides members with the opportunity to deepen their relational and spiritual growth through small groups that provide caring support, prayer, and Bible study.

Assimilate—Strengthening the Ministry

Someone needs to focus on building the ministry team. The challenge of the Assimilation Leader is to strengthen the commitment of the members to the ministry. The Assimilation Leader believes an effective ministry attracts new members and communicates to others what the ministry offers. The reason for this role is to promote the ministry, recruit new members, and preserve the culture of the ministry. This element of leadership provides the members with recognition, appreciation, and ministry identification.

Manage—Steering the Ministry

Someone needs to focus on the direction and objective of the ministry. The challenge of the Ministry Leader is to inspire the members' commitment to the purpose of the ministry. The Ministry Leader knows an effective ministry has a vision worth sharing, inspiring objectives, and a strong culture. The reason for this role is to direct the efforts of the ministry and encourage the development of the ministry through its growth process. This element of leadership provides the members direction and leadership.

The *big* difference here is that the focus is not on ministry structure or methodology but on people who lead and participate in the ministry. Your team creates a ministry environment in which members can: (1) expand their capacity to serve, (2) foster the development of their unique design; (3) get connected in caring relationships; (4) stimulate their capacity to learn; and (5) be challenged to increase the collective faith of the ministry to accomplish its mission.

The primary purpose is to build effective ministries through effective people, in order to magnify the performance of their service and overcome the barriers to the next level of the church's growth. The secondary purpose is to move existing ministries from a single-leader structure to a team-leadership structure and its accompanying values.

Function	Role	Purpose	Focus	Worker's Need	Performance Indicator
Train	Training Leader	Sharpens the Ministers	Skills	Enhancement	Quality of Service
Encourage	Shepherd Leader	Shepherds the Ministers	Support	Encouragement	Quality of Relationships
Assimilate	Assimilation Leader	Shapes the Ministers	Synergy	Expression	Quality of Team
Manage	Ministry Director	Steers the Ministry	Supervision	Exciting Vision	Quality of the Mission

Tapping the leadership potential of members already serving in ministry broadens the base of people carrying the load of ministry leadership. Fostering new ministry dreams unleashes the creativity the Holy Spirit has placed within God's people. Establishing sound guidelines for launching new ministries helps ensure those ministries will have a lasting impact on the church and community. Building new ministries on a T.E.A.M. leadership concept gives them great stability. Using the T.E.A.M. concept also makes it very clear when the "hold" should be over and the "release" initiated in the lives of your up-and-coming leaders.

Leading from the tilt isn't easy. We want to hold on to people far longer than we should. How qualified do you think the disciples were when Jesus gave them the Great Commission just before he ascended into heaven? Leading from the tilt means catch and release.

CHAPTER THIRTEEN

Remaining on Course

"New wine calls for new wineskins." —Mark 2:22b NLT

When I turned sixteen, all I could think about was getting my driver's license. I studied hard for the written exam—and actually did very well—but when it came to the actual driving test, my score was decidedly lower.

The night before I was to take the test, my mom's car with the automatic transmission broke down, and I had to use my dad's car. His had a stick shift. Well, let's just say I hadn't practiced much with a stick, but I did my best. Unfortunately, my best wasn't very good. During the grueling fifteen-minute drive I ground the gears several times.

Have you ever heard someone grind the gears of a transmission? Have you ever done it yourself? The sound of grinding gears still rings in my ears! Although I'm not by any stretch of the imagination a mechanic, just looking at a set of gears shows how they are intended to fit together in a very specific way and work together smoothly. You can understand that when gears aren't operating the way they were designed, a lot of stress is created and the whole car ends up being less effective than it should be.

Astoundingly, I did well enough to pass. But in the process I damaged Dad's transmission. The gears didn't operate as they were made to and as they had before I took the test. The members of the body of Christ are designed to fit together in a very specific way and to work together smoothly for God's glory (Romans 12:4-6) just like the gears in a well-designed transmission. As a leader, you not only have to make sure your ministry team is functioning smoothly, but you also have to monitor how well you are doing as a leader.

From time to time, the gears of your ministry are going to start to grind. It might simply be from normal wear and tear, or maybe you didn't make a shift very smoothly. Whatever the reason, your ministry—like a transmission—has to be adjusted from time to time for it to keep working the way God intended. If you want to experience all the marvelous dimensions of the empowering ministry God created you for, your ministry needs to be continually refined—and your spirit needs to be occasionally realigned with God's plan and purpose for you.

What type of team do you want to lead? What type of leader will you be? You can build a flourishing, highly functioning team that will want to follow your lead and fulfill the goals God has called you to set for his glory. For that to happen, you must regularly adjust the gears of your ministry to keep it operating properly. Most of the time, the changes are minor. But sometimes you have to create something entirely new. Change happens constantly—in people, in culture, in ministries and churches. That means new needs and opportunities arise that you may not have a mechanism to deal with. Or it means a way of ministering that used to work doesn't work anymore. Or perhaps God does something new in the life of your church. Jesus said, "New wine calls for new wineskins" (Mark 2:22b NLT). The need to change, for you to change as well as the ministry, is inevitable.

We must always be in a mode of improving our existing ministries and methods and, when needed, creating new ones. The point is that you never stop taking inventory. You must embrace the idea of constantly refining and enhancing your ministry. Yesterday's success—even today's victory—must not be allowed to get in the way of what God wants to do tomorrow.

If you want to remain on course, you need to be continually looking ahead and anticipating the changes your audience is and will be experiencing in their lives—their jobs, their neighborhoods, and their families. Your children and especially your grandchildren will grow up in a world you are not familiar with—just look at the world your grandparents grew up in! My grandmother was born in 1885. When we would visit I marveled at the fact that she knew real cowboys and Indians. She was thirty-five when women got the right to vote. When she was a youngster, airplanes hadn't been invented, freeways didn't exist, and America hadn't yet been through two World Wars. Now, on the other hand, my grandchildren don't know a world in which television didn't exist, they learn to use computers in preschool, and they use cell phones to call Nana and me.

Remaining on course requires that you continually adapt, upgrade, and renew your perspective on ministry. You mustn't lock into a tried-and-true paradigm. You will only turn yourself into a fossil. Thank God the word of God doesn't change! Only his mercies are new every morning!

The Place of Prayer

When we focus on refining our ministries, we tend to train the spotlight on better methods. We look around to see who is experiencing success in one aspect or another, and we adopt their methods. In so doing, not only have we made the mistake of thinking that methods developed in other contexts will work in ours, but we have missed God's priority in advancing his kingdom.

In *Power Through Prayer*, E. M. Bounds describes ministry as something that constantly stretches us, even strains us, to provide new tools, practices, and methods to advance the kingdom. However, he also recognizes that men are God's method, and though the church may be looking for better methods, God is looking for better people. In Ezekiel 22:30, the Lord said he looked—in vain—for someone who would "stand in the gap" (NLT) and provide leadership, but he found no one.

God is looking for leaders, and the secret to great leadership lies in the heart. The Bible says, "The eyes of the LORD search the whole earth in order to strengthen those whose hearts are fully committed to him" (2 Chronicles 16:9a NLT). When our ministries need to be realigned with God's priorities, the process begins in our hearts as we submit ourselves to the Lord in prayerful communion.

When the prophet Nehemiah faced the challenge of rebuilding the wall around Jerusalem, he didn't form a committee or commission a white paper. The first thing he did was to get alone with God. He prayed because he knew the task before him could be accomplished only if he was totally dependent on God and committed to doing it God's way, rather than following the path that seemed right to him.

We would all pray more if we realized that the task before us is too great for our own strength. We would pray more if we realized how inadequate our own understanding and insight are for the challenge we face. We collapse under the burden of stress because we fail to seek the Lord's plan and his power. God's promise to Jeremiah was "Call to Me and I will answer you, and I will tell you great and mighty things, which you do not know" (Jeremiah 33:3 NASB).

When we acknowledge in prayer who God is and confess who we are, God begins to realign us with his plan for our future. When we place our confidence in God's desire to make himself known among the nations and commit ourselves to join him in the specific actions he wants to take (not the ones we may want to take), God has an opportunity to open the doors of heaven and turn his dreams into our reality.

Pause right now and praise God for all he has done and is doing in your life and your ministry. Just as we all too often do in our personal prayers, we leaders have a habit of sharing with God all of our problems rather than starting with a great praise report. Some years ago Bruce and I were in Moscow negotiating a conference of great spiritual significance for the Russian army. You don't know Bruce, but he is a man of prayer. While I do believe in the power of prayer and pray often, Bruce's commitment to prayer is so much greater than mine. If I err, it is on the side of being too much a man of action with too little prayer.

We had just finished a meeting in the Ministry of Defense Building, their equivalent of the Pentagon. The meeting had not gone well, and it looked like the opportunity to address the top six hundred generals in the Russian army was not going to happen. We paused on the steps outside. It was nearly winter and bitterly cold. We all voiced our disappointment that our problems seemed too great to overcome. Then Bruce said, "Let's pray." And we did. Right there with all these uniforms walking past us up and down the stairs.

Then Bruce did a very strange thing. He said to me, "Jeff, God spoke to me and told me you need to get back in there and reopen negotiations while I pray. I don't know how you are even going to get past the guard, but there it is; now go do it."

"So, what did you say to God, 'Here am I, Lord; send Jeff'?" I replied. Back in I went and after a very long time, we got our conference and later our fifteen minutes of fame on CNN. Bruce and I both prayed through the ordeal; he in his gift of faith and I in my gift of action.

If the ministry is going to remain on course, it must be undergirded by prayer. Certainly, you will be praying, but in addition make sure you have a pastor's prayer team made up of people gifted in prayer who will undergird you throughout the many days you will be busy with those things that really need someone like Bruce standing out in the cold crying out to God on your behalf.

Taking Care of Self

Making minor adjustments while steering your car isn't a big deal, and it can keep you from crashing. But constantly evaluating your ministry and making corrections is time-consuming. Sometimes it can be very uncomfortable. Hard as it is to ask other people to make changes, it is always harder to accept the changes you as a leader need to make in yourself. But it must be done.

A leader who is out of alignment can't fine-tune either his ministry or his members. As difficult and important as it is to monitor your ministry and volunteers, it is far more important to evaluate how you are doing as a leader and keep yourself aligned.

During my time in ministry, I have learned that evaluation and transformation take training. Have you ever left a conference all fired up, saying to yourself, "I'm going to do that"? I've walked out of the sanctuary after an inspiring sermon, promising, "I'm *going* to be a better husband." I wake up the next morning, thinking, *This is the day I get it right like never before!* But no matter how hard I try my, old habits reassert themselves. I don't change overnight, at least not that first day.

Training takes time and effort, but the rewards are great. Like marathon runners endure the momentary disciplining of their body for the ultimate reward of winning the race, ministers endure spiritual discipline because it holds promise for this life and the life to come (1 Timothy 4:8). Here are a series of healthy spiritual habits for you to build into your life—daily, weekly, and monthly. These are just one man's ideas, and the goal is not to fit into them but to use them as a way to evaluate your life. Better yet, to make sure your gears are not grinding, develop your own way.

Daily Habits

1. Worship God. The Bible tells us to place ourselves before God as an act of worship: "I urge you, brothers, in view of God's mercy, to offer your bodies as living sacrifices, holy and pleasing to God—this is your spiritual act of worship"

(Romans 12:1 NIV). By this act of surrender, we allow God to take full ownership of our lives each day.

Surrendering to God is the habit with greatest benefit because honoring God with your life is what pleases him more than anything. A daily time of surrender allows you to review your life and be sure you have given everything to God.

2. Study God's word. Computer programmers have a saying: "Garbage in, garbage out." That means software can't perform with excellence if the code input by the programmer is shoddy. The same thing is true of our spiritual lives. The magazines we read, the music we listen to, the shows we watch on TV—these things and many others have a positive or negative effect on our lives as ministers and leaders.

Before Christ came into my life, I allowed all sorts of unhealthy garbage into my mind. But when I opened my life to Christ, I began changing everything I listened to, watched, and read. And over time, my desires and habits changed as well. I knew that if I was to experience God's best for my life, I had to allow only the very best into my mind.

The best food for your mind, of course, is God's word. The Bible is God's road map for your life, the only thing you can rely upon as totally trustworthy. God challenged the Israelites of Joshua's day to study his word continually, to "meditate on it day and night" (Joshua 1:8 NLT). If you are going to experience the empowering ministry God has in store for you, you also need to study and apply God's truth to your life. We need to study the Bible—God's love letter to us—every day, a habit rooted in our love for Christ, not an obligation to follow someone's rule. When we put in the best, the best is what will come out in our attitudes and actions.

3. Quiet your heart. If your life is anything like mine, it's pretty fast-paced, even hectic, most of the time. I have to be constantly reminded to slow down and walk *with* God, not run out ahead of him. Only when we are "still in the presence of the LORD, and wait patiently for him to act" (Psalm 37:7a NLT) do we have any hope of understanding what he is trying to say to us.

Being silent is not an easy habit to develop; but if we are to walk with God effectively, it is a habit we must develop. We need to take time on a daily basis to silence our hearts before God. With so many obligations, distractions, and activities competing for our attention, being still before God requires serious effort on our part. We need to commit to doing whatever it takes to silence ourselves before God.

Weekly Habits

1. Rest your body and soul. God felt so strongly about the importance of honoring him through rest that he included it in the Ten Commandments: "Remember the Sabbath day by keeping it holy. Six days you shall labor and do all your work, but the seventh day is a Sabbath to the LORD your God. On it you shall not do any work" (Exodus 20:8–10a NIV). The word *sabbath* actually means "to catch one's breath."

Too many of us, however, take God's Sabbath command as mere suggestion. How loving is a God who insists his children do something so completely unproductive? I hope you'll do God the honor of following his example and set aside one day each week to rest.

2. Love God's people. If any animal ever needed shepherding, it's sheep. Left to their own devices, sheep will wander into all sorts of danger. Jesus used the image of a shepherd to describe how he loved and cared for his people, even at great risk to himself (John 10:11). After his resurrection, Jesus told Peter that if he really loved him, he should feed his sheep (John 21:15-17). The minister who wants to see God empowering the entire congregation should strive to maximize the many opportunities he or she has each week to care for and serve God's people. Gentle, caring, loving servanthood shows our love for God by loving his people.

3. Spend time with people who don't know God. Pastors and ministry leaders focused on meeting the many demands of ministry can forget the most basic expectation Jesus has of his followers—bringing others along with them as disciples. The Great Commission is very plain that we are to "go and make disciples of all nations" (Matthew 28:19 NIV). Jesus didn't say that God was glorified by starting many new programs or holding many meetings, but by our bearing much fruit (John 15:8). I know you already know this, but we all need reminding. I do, too.

If you have gotten slack about telling others about the difference Christ has made in your life, challenge yourself to do that at least once a week. If you have never been in the habit of seeking out opportunities to share the good news of salvation in Jesus Christ, it's a habit you need to start!

Monthly Habits

1. Unplug from life—plug into God. When was the last time you got away from all the busyness of life to just be alone with your heavenly Father? If you haven't done that recently, mark your calendar now to spend at least half a day alone with God. Too busy, you say? Even as busy as Jesus was, he still made time alone with God a priority. Very early in the morning, while it was still dark, he would get up and go off to a solitary place to pray (Mark 1:35).

If you are going to stay aligned with God's purpose for your ministry, you must spend uninterrupted quality time with him. Find a place where you can disconnect from the world and your daily routine—a retreat center or park, a hotel at the beach or a cabin in the mountains. The location isn't nearly as important as the attitude of your heart. Use the escape from the noise and interruptions of life to take inventory of your ministry and reflect on God's purpose and direction for your ministry. If you do this on a monthly basis, you will be astonished at the difference it makes in your ministry the rest of the time.

2. Chart your progress. Self-evaluation is essential if you are to stay aligned with God's purpose and direction for your ministry. While others play a critical role in that process, you can gain helpful insights by asking yourself the right questions, especially if you do this as part of a solitude retreat with God.

Here are four key questions to ask yourself:

1. Praises—What can I celebrate in my life right now?
2. Problems—What opportunities for change do I see?
3. People—What connections can I make?
4. Plans—What new ideas need to be developed?

3. Shape up. Even if we don't have a formal leadership title, each of us has the opportunity to influence others—at home, work, or anytime in our daily lives. To all those people, you are a leader, and God has designed you uniquely to show them how to follow Christ more faithfully and effectively.

Being a leader means being a continual learner. None of us ever arrive at a point where we are as good as God can make us. Determine as part of your monthly schedule to sharpen your understanding of your S.H.A.P.E. and strengthen your usefulness to God. The Bible says, "If the ax is dull and its edge unsharpened, more strength is needed but skill will bring success" (Ecclesiastes 10:10 NIV). God deserves your best, so make it a priority to be continually learning how to better serve him and others.

Give Others Permission

As critical as self-evaluation is, the problem is that you really can't do it yourself. As a leader, you have to muster the courage to ask the people you lead to tell you how you are doing as a leader.

Very few of us ever do that at all. Even fewer do it regularly. No matter how uncomfortable it is, however, asking others for their evaluation of you is an absolute necessity if you are going to be a leader who empowers others for ministry. You must ask the tough questions about yourself, and you have to give your team permission to speak truth into your life. Otherwise, you will never know what needs changing until it is too late. To get that kind of feedback, you have to ask questions. I encourage you to ask your team members these four questions on a regular basis:

What is one way I can improve as a leader? One of my team members replied to this question, "You're traveling a lot. It would be great to know where you are during those times if we need to reach you." She was saying she needed better communication. Another person said, "I need more details about what I'm doing in this ministry." He was saying he needed more structure—knowing the expectations and boundaries. He didn't feel like he had everything he needed from me.

What is one thing you need from me so you can succeed in your role? As I said before, I have a deep-seated need to be in control. Sometimes I dip down into the details, and that can keep my team members from succeeding. My associate has had to tell me, "Get out of my kitchen! Stop messing with me! Trust me." I'm learning that I've got to give up control and trust that he's got it. Something about your leadership may be keeping your team from succeeding. They must have your permission to tell you what it is.

Am I maximizing your strengths and passions? As the team's leader, I have to make sure 80 percent of each member's job is in his or her sweet spot. To that end, we are constantly fine-tuning the members' roles, trying to get them into their niche. My sweet spot is not theirs, and theirs is not mine. If we are going to see the kind of Empowering Ministry God wants to turn loose in our church, we have got to be sure that we are working with him to maximize the strengths and passions he has placed in the hearts of our people.

If you were the leader of this team, what would you do differently? This is a hard question, but I challenge you to ask it. Open yourself up to receiving feedback and even tell them you don't want to hear any praises. Tell your team you want to hear about something you can improve on.

Remember, there is always the rabble. Though feedback is helpful, there will always be those who murmur about you, the team, the ministry, the sky, and the grass—virtually anything. Make sure you have a thick enough skin to not take things personally and to filter out what is not constructive. If you receive anonymous letters or e-mails, don't respond. People with the courage of their convictions—the ones who will give you the best feedback—will identify themselves. You can ignore the rest.

Evaluate Your Team

Once you have asked your team members to evaluate you, it's important to ask them to evaluate themselves and the ministry. Sometimes evaluation is a frightening thing to team members. It shouldn't be—and won't be if it is conducted in the right spirit.

We have to remember that we are all parts of Christ's body, all members of God's family. Our evaluation times need to be conducted in a spirit of mutual care and concern, as well as accountability. Only then do team members feel free to share the issues that prevent God's Spirit from empowering the ministry.

In our staff updates, we ask ourselves a number of questions—some related to the broader ministry and some personal in nature. All of them are important if we are going to have the kind of close relationship a team needs to succeed.

- How are we doing at surrendering?
- How are we doing at embracing?
- How are we doing at releasing?
- How are we doing at valuing?
- How are we doing at enhancing?

- What kind of progress have we made?
- What praises do we have to report?
- How are we doing with that principle in our life?
- Where have we found God working to help us live a surrendered life?
- Are there any problems in the way?
- What are our plans?

Evaluate the Ministry

It's not enough for you and your team to evaluate yourselves. We don't have the perspective needed to see everything that needs to be adjusted. The view a manager sees from the front office is different from what workers see on the assembly line. You also must welcome feedback from your volunteers and members.

In corporate America, collecting feedback is sometimes called TQM—Total Quality Management. The goal of TQM is to create an environment that welcomes feedback and ideas. Businesses typically use this feedback to fine-tune their services and look for new ways to meet the needs of customers.

The church, of course, is not a corporation; it's an organism— the body of Christ. But if we truly are putting others first, we must welcome feedback from our volunteers in ministry to ensure we are helping them succeed in their roles. Some of the greatest ideas to strengthen your church will come from your members and your volunteers.

You have to be very intentional, however, about creating an environment that welcomes feedback. Volunteers and members won't normally take the initiative to share ideas—except, of course, the complainers. If you don't have an environment that welcomes feedback, you aren't going to receive helpful perspective on how to improve your service.

There are a number of tools you can use to obtain feedback: phone calls, e-mails, print surveys, and focus groups, for example. Sometimes, however, people are reluctant to respond candidly. A solution to that is to use an online tool like Survey-Monkey or Zoomerang. You can create a page on the Internet that allows you to get quality data while giving people the anonymity that allows them to respond candidly. Now, I know we recommended ignoring anonymous feedback. However, that recommendation had the "poison pen" communication in mind. What anonymous surveys allow you to do is identify trends or perspectives that are helpful to understand. What most of us experience is our reality regardless of the good intentions of others. What we want to know, good, bad, or ugly, is what is the reality of our audience. Sites like SurveyMonkey have plenty of statistical means for weeding out the malcontents and ax grinders, so don't be afraid to try it.

Welcoming feedback and new ideas requires willingness on your part to embrace and help initiate changes when someone makes an excellent suggestion. If your members never know that you listen to them, they are going to feel like their feedback fell on deaf ears. You must not only invite ideas, you have to *ignite* ideas—by allowing them to come to fruition.

A Final Word

We hope in reading this book you have caught a new vision of yourself as an Empowering Leader who has realigned in ministry to release God's people to empowering ministries of their own. Be sure you take the long view of the process so you won't get discouraged if things don't radically change overnight. Chances are they won't.

Right now, right this minute—could you lace up your sneakers, warm up and stretch for a few minutes, and go run a marathon? Only a handful of people could do that—and neither one of us is one of them. But if each of us spent the next twelve months training, we could show up a year from today and take our best shot at running a marathon. We still might not last the entire distance, but we could all do better a year from now than we could today, if we discipline ourselves to reach that goal. It's a matter of training—and training takes time.

Give yourself permission to dream, "What kind of leader could I be a year from now? How much progress could I make this next year if I trained myself and pulled a team around me for support?"

The last thing you should do is close this book and say, "I'm going to do everything differently today." Transformation doesn't happen overnight. We have to get into a process of training that will, over time, get us where we want to go in ministry.

From the outside, some churches seem to be smoothly functioning, well-oiled ministry machines. For most churches, ours included, from the inside they don't look all that efficient! And even the best of them didn't get to their level of success overnight. It took years and years of experimenting—trial and error, failure and success—to get where they are today. Your experience isn't likely to be any different.

The challenge for you is to start with yourself. Don't try to make giant leaps. Take little steps. Develop an action plan that sets out small goals you realistically can achieve over the next thirty, sixty, and ninety days. Rather than thinking you've got to go back and change everything next week, leave this book with a mind-set of *training*, not trying.

Pull out a sheet of paper and list three small things you can do that will move you in the direction of realigning your ministry and empowering your church for kingdom service. Think of these goals in terms of the time it will take for you to accomplish them:

1. Over the next thirty days, I will . . .
2. Over the next sixty days, I will . . .
3. Over the next ninety days, I will . . .

Common Leadership Wisdom: *Well-trained leaders* are needed to guide the ministry to fruifulness.

The Tilt: *Empowered leaders* on an empowered pathway are difference makers in the kingdom of God.

Every day, you have a new opportunity to make a little more headway into realigning your ministry and releasing your people. As you lead by example, over time and through the power of the Holy Spirit, people will begin to understand what you are talking about. They will catch a vision of Empowering Ministry and get on board. They will see that it's working. In time, it becomes less of a program and more of a culture, a DNA pattern that reproduces itself over and over and over.

You may not have a corps of volunteers to start with. You may not even have anyone else on your ministry team. In that case, "focus down." Start by serving the people you do have in your circle of influence. Show them what it means to realign your vision and release people to ministry. A year from now, you'll find you have more volunteers and that you're personally doing more of what you are designed to do. More ministry will be getting done. Just start where you can in your circle of influence and give yourself enough time to make some real progress.

Isaiah captures what all of us long to be in ministry when he says, "A man shall be as an hiding place from the wind, and a covert from the tempest; as rivers of water in a dry place, as the shadow of a great rock in a weary land" (Isaiah 32:2 KJV). This is the ultimate tilt—empowered leaders filled with hope making a difference for the kingdom of God.

Now, there is just one more concept to cover.

CHAPTER FOURTEEN

Spiritual Transformation

If anyone is in Christ, he is a new creature; the old things passed away;
behold, new things have come.
—2 Corinthians 5:17 NASB

My job—God's job. It is tough to keep these things straight sometimes. In our efforts to be fruitful it is easy to focus on perspective, method, and process to the point that we lose sight of a fundamental truth in ministry. I can't change anyone. People must choose change for themselves. Then God transforms them.

As a university chaplain I had the chance to influence the lives of many students with the gospel message. My heart longed to see these young men and women come to know Jesus Christ in a real and personal manner just as I did. Only, I was convinced I could make it happen. Thoroughly trained in evangelism, skilled in apologetics, successful in discipleship—I knew my powers of convincingness would win even the most secular, hardened heart! Clearly, I had a lot to learn.

One day after I spoke at a student rally one young man showed interest and agreed to meet with me weekly to discuss the claims of the gospel. We further agreed that we would read the Gospel of John and make that the basis of our discussions but that anything was fair game. Let's call him Brad.

When Brad showed up for our first discussion he had in tow his sidekick. Let's call him Little Brad because over time it became obvious he was a clone of Brad, almost as if Brad had his own personal sycophant. I didn't think much of Little Brad. He agreed with everything coming out of Brad's mouth like a pet parrot. But they both kept showing up faithfully week after week, and eventually Little Brad just faded into the background. I was after the ringleader, the strong one, and I was going to make it happen!

The time came when it seemed Brad was ready to commit his life to Christ. We were in the student center sitting at a small square table. Brad was opposite me and Little Brad sat to my right. At that hour of the morning not too many people were around, a good time to "cross the finish line" with this guy.

"Well," I said, "if there isn't any reason you should not receive Christ, why don't we pray right now and you can invite him into your heart?" Brad exploded! "I am NOT going to pray! Jesus may be who he claims to be, but I want nothing to do with him!" He said more, but it is not worth repeating here.

As I sat there struggling with how I could have missed this antagonism and underlying rejection, a soft-spoken Little Brad spoke up. "What do I say?" he asked. As I looked over, my second surprise came. Little Brad, with head bowed and hands folded like he was saying grace at the dinner table, wanted to know how to receive Christ.

We prayed together with Brad looking on. This silent participant in all those conversations that I practically ignored got the message. He chose to become a child of God, and before my very eyes Jesus Christ spiritually transformed him. That was my first lesson in spiritual transformation. I can't change anyone. They must choose change for themselves. Then God transforms them. I don't know what ever happened to Brad after that. But Little Brad became Todd and grew up to be a man of faith and courage with a testimony I admire.

More lessons came through the years. As a change agent my training and experience extended from people to groups and then to companies, corporations, denominations, and eventually international conglomerates. My sweet spot is influencing change in people, not systems, and success has been built around this fundamental truth. It is a frustrating axiom—we can create the environment, we can coach for change and lead through change, we can motivate, inspire, equip, and educate—but we cannot make people change.

In this book we have talked about doing things differently, giving conventional wisdom just a slight tilt that makes the difference between something familiar, tried, and usual and something powerful, energetic, new, and revitalizing. We have talked about change more or less from our perspective. Now it is time for one last tilt. Let's talk about change from God's perspective.

Change and Transformation Are Not the Same

What causes plants to grow toward the light? Why do flowers follow the march of the sun across the sky only to relax, turn back, and await the next sunrise to do it all over again? The answer is easy: They are designed to face the warmth and light of the sun. When those first rays of sunlight strike them, something happens and they begin to change position. A response grows and continues for as long as the sun shines. That is a great picture of change. Change is always a response to something.

Change doesn't take place in a vacuum. There is always a stimulus, a reason. People are like that, too. We change in response to things all the time. It's cold outside, so we put a coat on. We are hungry, so we get something to eat. We are late for an appointment, so we drive faster. We are hurt by someone, so we withdraw from her or we become angry at him. We need to lose weight, so we go on a diet and begin to

Common Leadership Wisdom: Continuing relevance in ministry requires *change*.

The Tilt: Continuing relevance in ministry requires *spiritual transformation*—change and transformation are not the same thing.

exercise. We recognize unproductive thoughts and change our attitude. Someone loves us and our heart fills with comfort. We may even love him or her back.

No matter if the change is intentional or natural, physical, emotional, or spiritual, it is a response to something. In the workplace we reward people to create incentives for changed productivity. At home we discipline our children with clear consequences in hopes their behavior will change. At school we change our study habits to get a better grade. Obviously, employees, children, and students of all ages don't necessarily always choose to make the desired changes. Some change happens in response to conscious decision. Sometimes change is a natural or automatic response like shielding our eyes from bright light, being afraid of the dark, or avoiding people we don't like. Still, change is a response to some real or perceived stimulus and isn't the creation of something totally new. That would be transformation.

When Todd accepted Christ, something happened. Everyone could see the difference in him as the days and weeks went by. What was Todd responding to that we all perceived as a change? A transformation had taken place in his soul. This was something he had decided he needed, something he asked for, something he invited—but not something he had any power to make happen. Jesus transformed him in the core of his being and made something brand-new, something that never existed before, come into being. That is Paul's point in 2 Corinthians 5:17 when he says we have become a new creature and that the old is gone, all things have become new.

Now, clearly there is a bit of a paradox regarding change. On one hand, we cannot make someone change, while on the other hand we have suggested that we can influence change in others' lives by providing a stimulus they respond to—an incentive, a consequence, or some other reason. Marriage provides a great illustration of how this works.

Suppose Nancy prefers to hang the toilet paper rolls with the paper coming off the top in front, but I prefer the paper to hang and come off the back of the roll. She insists that I change my habit and use her method. For whatever reason (knowing that how the paper hangs is not the real issue), I dig my heels in and refuse to change. The more that Nancy insists, the more entrenched I become in my own opinion. We have all been in a situation like this with someone over some issue at one time or another.

Suddenly, Nancy decides it is okay to be different. She quits riding me about the matter, even thanks me for replacing the rolls. In other ways, over other matters, she becomes less insistent and more flexible, communicating that being different in some things is just fine. Her demeanor and attitude evoke a response in me. I want to be more cooperative and, as a favor to her, begin hanging the rolls according to her preference because my natural response to her changed attitude is to please her. She couldn't force change upon me, but her attitude change evoked a response in me.

Understanding the relationship between spiritual transformation and change is important. If we want to see God work in our lives and through our lives in the lives of other people and in our ministry, we need to agree that the Holy Spirit must inhabit our ministries. Only as the Spirit spiritually transforms us and our ministry can real growth take place. Otherwise, the changes that we see occurring will be nothing more than empty mechanics built around our human abilities to organize, lead, motivate, and train others. When we are no longer around pumping energy into things, they will die—but if the Holy Spirit is transforming the ministry, the results will be lasting, and the contribution of our gifts, skills, talents, and abilities will no longer be empty mechanics. They will take on new power in astounding ways!

Spiritual transformation is God's job; influencing change is my job—and they are not the same thing. So, what does spiritual transformation look like from God's perspective?

People Must Choose Change

When Nancy's attitude and behavior began to change I was presented with a choice. I could respond naturally to her influence or I could resist the inclination to change. Often resistance is natural and healthy, sort of a built-in check-and-balance. Even Paul resisted the Lord Jesus Christ. "It is hard for you to kick against the goads," Jesus told Paul (Acts 26:14 NASB). There was a lesson tied up in his resistance that is important to understand.

When young oxen were trained for the yoke, they were harnessed just in front of the cart. The oxen would resist, kicking out and pulling this way and that at first. However, along the crosspiece on the tongue was a series of sharp stakes positioned in such a way that the oxen, when kicking, would prick or goad themselves on the points. Soon the oxen chose surrender and learned to control their movements. A farmer plowing behind a young ox unused to the harness would carry a long stick sharpened at one end and use it in the same manner. Paul's resistance was a "kicking out"of sorts that kept running into the goads Jesus had placed in his way. Paul could have chosen to remain unchanged, to keep fighting, to stick with his plan; but he didn't. He chose to surrender. Without that choice there would have been no change forthcoming.

When it comes to spiritual maturity or spiritual growth in ourselves or in our ministry, we have the same choice to make. Will we be open to change? Will we welcome something new and different into our lives? Will we choose to change as the Spirit leads and God wills? Looking at this same moment from God's perspective, the question becomes will we chose to surrender? Following is a short self-test that may help you assess your willingness to surrender.

These two columns list characteristics that we all experience to some degree. On each row circle the description that fits you more often than the description next to it. Remember, we all exhibit both traits but usually have a preference for one over the other.

I am comfortable with things remaining the same and don't enjoy surprises.	I welcome change and enjoy being surprised.
If I believe I am right about something, I will usually lobby others to come around to my way of thinking.	If I believe I am right about something, I will still listen to other opinions and will modify my own accordingly.
I am very competitive and strive to win.	I am somewhat competitive and like to win.
When I have lost unfairly, it is harder to be a good sport.	When I have lost unfairly, I can still be a good sport.
Sometimes I envy what other people have.	Success of others always makes me happy.
I do worry sometimes about being replaced in someone else's heart.	I am secure when my friends change and move on.
I sometimes find myself negotiating with God.	I am always excited about doing God's will when I am confident about what it is.

If you circled more of the characteristics in the left-hand column than the right, surrender may be more difficult for you. You may have some resistance to choosing change for yourself when something in life comes along and requires that choice on your part. One of the best things you can do when that happens is not to focus on the choice but to ask yourself instead, "What is it that God wants me to be surrendered to?" Try to look at change from God's perspective.

We Create the Environment

We don't always see things clearly for what they really are, especially when it comes to ourselves. "Clark" often gives me tips about ministry. He believes that he is a popular speaker and fancies himself an accomplished disciple maker. Clark knows a veritable list of Who's Who in Christendom and reminds people often of those connections. In short, he believes himself to be pretty close to the ideal minister.

The truth is very different. Sent home from the mission field for insubordination, Clark failed in his first attempt at being a pastor, driving a thriving church into oblivion. He and his wife create constant conflict and division in whatever ministry they are involved in, and he has never been invited a second time to speak anywhere. Yes, Clark does know a lot of people—most of whom do not prefer his company. Yet, Clark has this uncanny ability to see all of this through his own special lens. My job was to change his filter. Oh joy. I get to work with someone who believes he is being rejected for his righteousness when it is really his self-righteousness and arrogance that is the problem!

What Jesus sees is a child of God. Someone he died for and someone he loves very, very much. Clark is flawed but no more unredeemable than I am . . . or you are. What Jesus sees is someone in need of a reality check, someone who needs an opportunity to choose to be different. What is the best environment to create in which this can occur? How do we take the obstacles of human instrumentality out of the way as much as possible so the Holy Spirit can work?

Paul, talking to the Corinthians in part about their unrealistic self-appraisal, describes us as looking into a mirror darkly and says that if we take the veil off our face we will be able to see ourselves in Jesus as we truly are . . . and be transformed more and more into his image. There it is again, the word *metamorphosis*. When we choose to embrace reality, God can do that marvelous work in our hearts, making us different than we are,

new and improved! God sees in Clark a life that needs transformation. My job is to help create the environment that can
best enable Clark to come to grips with reality in his life by facing the mirror—Christ. Then Clark's ability to change will
be limited only by his ability to embrace reality.

Through a number of personal coaching sessions with Clark
we identified what his design and calling were, as well as what
his purpose on this earth consisted of, and the revelation galva-
nized him. It wasn't as easy as that single sentence makes it
seem. There were uncomfortable conversations about how others experienced him. From time to time we would use breakthrough tools to provide independent information that often met
with disagreement on his part. Clark even argued over his spiritual gifts, passion, abilities, and talents because they didn't
match his perception of himself.

Clark wanted to repair his marriage, and that led to marriage
counseling for him and his wife. He wanted to further his education and eventually finished a master's in business administration. One requirement placed upon him in this process was to
get and keep a job, any job, and become a responsible provider
for his family. You can imagine why consistent employment may
have been a challenge. Clark needed to face up to a lot of things
in his life that, if ignored, would compromise his ability to
embrace the truth and realize his purpose. He needed more than
just information, a checklist, or a road map. So, we worked with
Clark for more than three years creating the environment that
built the missing foundation in his life.

A coach creates an environment conducive to self-discovery
and focuses people on what is real in their lives first before moving on to what is hoped for or imagined. Successful coaching
explores, as you can imagine in Clark's case, self-image at deeply
personal levels and anticipates that resistance is to be expected.

Clark is an unusual example. Sometimes all you will need in
your ministry is a change in climate and not a radical change in
culture. Sometimes people simply need a forgiving environment

to experiment in, permission to fail, or freedom to be creative. It may take very little time to see a difference, or it may be a longer process as it was with Clark. Whatever it is that is needed, creating the environment that enables people to align their goals, expectations, and desires with those of the ministry in the context of their design, calling, and purpose only sets the stage for the real drama.

God Transforms People

Sometimes change is impossibly hard because we can't get outside ourselves to see where it is that God wants to take us. When we do get outside ourselves, we often discover that our spiritual transformation has more to do with a journey than it does with a moment.

Song of Solomon 2:10 presents an expression that is both beautiful and rare: "My beloved responded and said to me, 'Arise, my darling, my beautiful one, and come along'" (NASB). The primitive root behind the idea of "come along" means to go toward yourself as you travel. Odd, but that is the expression. It fashions in the imagination a picture of a journey that moves you into the future in search of yourself, a journey that has only your benefit in view and not harm. Sounds a lot like Jeremiah 29:11, doesn't it? "'I know the plans that I have for you,' declares the LORD, 'plans for welfare and not for calamity to give you a future and a hope'" (NASB).

The only other place this specific concept appears is in Genesis 12:1-2: "The LORD said to Abram, 'Go forth from your country, and from your relatives and from your father's house, to the land which I will show you; and I will make you a great nation, and I will bless you, and make your name great; and so you shall be a blessing'" (NASB).

Abram was called to "go forth," to leave for some undesignated place and "go toward himself" in the journey. Imagine what this meant for Abram. Going toward himself meant he had to get outside his thinking; outside his society and culture; outside his training and education; outside his experience; outside his denomination, heritage, family; and even outside his own sinfulness.

What did God do along the way? He transformed Abram into Abraham. It took Abraham eighteen years to find himself. Abraham didn't do it. His family didn't do it. Those he met along the way didn't do it. God did it, and God used all those things in the warp and woof of what was happening in Abraham's life including the good, the bad, and the ugly. The journey is different for each of us. From God's perspective every person, every circumstance, every struggle, every victory is transformational—even though from our perspective it just feels like life. Our job is to help people with the journey. God's job is to make them different people.

People must choose change for themselves—we can shed some light on that for them. We create the environment—and can help them with the journey. God transforms people—we don't change them. That seems simple enough. Why, then, is it so hard to keep ourselves in check when it comes to the temptation to make them, force them, into our mold? Sometimes it is paternalism—we think we know what is best. Sometimes it is legalism—you have to follow the rules. Sometimes it is egotism—they have to follow us! Sometimes . . . sometimes it is a confusion of roles.

As a spiritual leader we need to be clear about many things, firm and unwavering, even directive. But when it comes to influencing change, the spiritual leader has a very clear role unlike other roles in the ministry. Notice the vocabulary used around passages of Scripture describing spiritual change in one fashion or another:

> Let us hold fast the confession of our hope without wavering, for He who promised is faithful; and let us consider how to stimulate one another to love and good deeds, not forsaking our own assembling together, as is the habit of some, but

encouraging one another; and all the more as you see the day drawing near. (Hebrews 10:23-25 NASB)

The change envisioned here is the continuing and increasing of love and good works. We are challenged to encourage or exhort one another in this regard, not demand it of each other.

The things which you have heard from me in the presence of many witnesses, entrust these to faithful men who will be able to teach others also. (2 Timothy 2:2 NASB)

The process of reproducing in others what Paul's life has demonstrated calls for change. Modeling is what is described, not manipulation.

He gave some as apostles, and some as prophets, and some as evangelists, and some as pastors and teachers, for the equipping of the saints for the work of service, to the building up of the body of Christ; until we all attain to the unity of the faith, and of the knowledge of the Son of God, to a mature man, to the measure of the stature which belongs to the fullness of Christ. (Ephesians 4:11-13 NASB)

Building up the body is all about change and moving forward with greater maturity. We are to equip others to do this and not force or compel them to engage in the work of service.

Paul's testimony before King Agrippa gives us insight into what Jesus' expectations are regarding change and transformation and our role:

While so engaged as I was journeying to Damascus with the authority and commission of the chief priests, at midday, O King, I saw on the way a light from heaven, brighter than the sun, shining all around me and those who were journeying with me. And when we had all fallen to the ground, I heard a voice saying to me in the Hebrew dialect, "Saul, Saul, why are you persecuting Me? It is hard for you to kick against the goads." And I said, "Who are You, Lord?" And the Lord said, "I am Jesus whom you are persecuting. But get up and stand on your feet; for this purpose I have appeared to you, to appoint you a minister and a witness not only to the things which you have seen, but also to the things in which I will appear to you; rescuing you from the Jewish people and from the Gentiles, to whom I am sending you, to open their eyes so that they may turn from darkness to light and from the dominion of Satan to God, that they may receive forgiveness of sins and an inheritance among those who have been sanctified by faith in Me." (Acts 26:12-18 NASB)

As a minister and a witness Paul was commissioned to *open their eyes,* leading to repentance, forgiveness of sin, and salvation; nothing less than the most significant change anyone can experience in life. The idea here is one of working toward enlightenment, insight, understanding—not brainwashing. It is the Holy Spirit that opens the mind and the heart, often using what we as servants and witnesses have communicated in the message of our walk and our talk. We are communicators, while the Holy Spirit is the convincer.

Clark is part of one of the churches mentioned earlier in this book needing a turnaround. The church had been in existence for some time but had grown to a place where its leaders valued their culture more than the commandments of the Lord. Clark and others were comfortable with and interested in perpetuating the status quo. The idea of "going" into the community, adapting their ministries as the needs of people changed in the region around the church, somehow escaped everyone's attention. Matthew 28:18-20 focuses our attention of continually making disciples as we go through life. The process grammatically described here is a continuing one with no recess, no interruption, and no status quo.

Now that church has grown to nearly five hundred members in two and a half years. People are coming to Christ nearly every week and not because there was an invitation from the pulpit. Did you hear that? Even when there is no invitation from the pulpit, people are coming to Christ. Now, that is evidence of a transformational ministry inhabited by the Holy Spirit!

When your ministry is reaching out and going deeper, everything takes on new life. Bibles studies, small groups, men's ministry, women's ministry, lay counseling, the homeless shelter, youth events, and everything else you have going on becomes the place where people are doing life together. It is in this crucible, not Saturday or Sunday morning, that the message of the gospel is lived out, practiced, modeled, tested, questioned, and tried on for size. The church service just becomes the place and time where commitment to the Savior is recognized publicly. This makes perfect sense. After all, it is God's church, God's body, and not our church.

When we get confused about these things, problems set in. We are so resourceful, have so many tools and aids at our disposal, and have such an advantage in excellent education and training that we can manufacture what looks like success without any real transformation taking place at all. All the more reason, then, to make sure we keep our roles distinguishable. We have our job; God has his. Paul describes this partnership well: "Walk by the Spirit, and you will not carry out the desire of the flesh. For the flesh sets its desire against the Spirit, and the Spirit against the flesh; for these are in opposition to one another, so that you may not do the things that you please. But if you are led by the Spirit, you are not under the Law" (Galatians 5:16-18 NASB). The Holy Spirit leads; we follow in obedience. He has his job, and I have my job. It is tough to keep these things straight sometimes.

Prayer

Late last night, around 10:30, I received a call from one of our elders. The elder had just read an article about church turnarounds and was so excited he couldn't wait until today to talk about it. The elder was convinced what this article described was exactly what we needed. Impatient but well-meaning, he was insistent that we plan an implementation immediately. I know you have had these kinds of conversations as well.

Here is what I told my friend: Don't be swayed by a single article. Do your homework and understand what is being discovered across the spectrum of church growth before you jump on something. Each church exists in a unique setting, and you have to understand who your ministry is to and who the community is that you serve in order to understand if your research is going to be applicable. One size does not fit all. Second, don't think about what to do before you have thought through what you need to pray.

This is the crux. We are so prepared to do something that we often don't even pray. Yet it is prayer that is so crucial to the success of our ministry. It is God who builds his church, not us. Notice the choice of words: "On this rock I will build My church, and the gates of Hades shall not prevail against it'" (Matthew 16:18 NKJV). Jesus builds his body, we don't! That would seem to suggest that a conversation with him would be important with regard to church growth.

Prayer is more than a tool for self-expression, not just about me or us, but about things much bigger than us—the kingdom and what God wants for our best. We have to pray before we act if we are ever going to discover that if we pray sometimes we will not have to act at all. The Holy Spirit doesn't fall on plans; he falls on people. What we have said here about practical tools and perspectives will not help you in the long run if you are not a person of prayer. We pray with you that through you, God would be pleased to build his church.

For those who find these stories, ideas, and tools helpful and would like to ask a question, make a comment, chat with the authors, or interact with your colleagues, please visit www.empoweringchurch.com.

Value-Driven Behaviors Card Sort

Copy each of the following values onto an index card that can be sorted easily. Place on the card first the name of the value and then the brief description of what this value looks like in action so that it can be easily and quickly read.

Knowledge

Spending time in the pursuit of knowledge, truth, and understanding

---

Put all the cards together so that you have a deck made up of all thirty-six values. Make as many decks as you need so that each person has a deck to sort.

Knowledge	Spending time in the pursuit of knowledge, truth, and understanding
Help Society	Contributing to the betterment of the world or community I live in

Affiliation	Being part of a company, organization, or work team that accepts me as a team member
Stability	Having a work routine and job duties that are largely predictable and not likely to change over a period of time
Public Contact	Having a lot of day-to-day interaction with people
Physical Challenge	Facing physical demands that I find rewarding
Recognition	Earning rewards or public acknowledgment for the quality of my work
Leadership	Having the opportunity to lead others through direction, influence, and motivation
Security	Feeling assured of keeping my job and a reasonable financial reward
Artistic	Producing work with aesthetic value; engaging in creative work in any of several art forms
Creative Expressions	Expressing in writing or verbally my ideas, reactions, and observations
Job Tranquillity	Avoiding work-related pressures and the "rat race"
Moral Fulfillment	Feeling that my work is contributing to a set of moral standards that I feel are very important
Status	Having a position that others—my friends, family, and community—respect and value

Excitement	Experiencing a high degree of (or frequent) excitement in the course of my work
Power and Authority	Having the ability to control the work activities and rewards for others
Work Alone	Doing projects by myself, without any significant amount of contact with others
High Earnings	Anticipating financial rewards that will allow me to purchase those things I consider essential and the luxuries of the life I wish to live
Mental Stimulation	Constantly using my mind and continuing to develop my intellect
Fast Pace	Working rapidly and in an environment with a lot of activity
Responsibility	Making decisions and controlling my work domain; overseeing projects and/or personnel
Decision Making	Having the power to decide courses of action, policies, and so on
Change and Variety	Having responsibilities and activities that frequently change in their content and/or setting
Independence	Determining the nature of my work without significant direction from others; setting my own direction rather than merely following orders
Pressure	Working under time pressure and/or having the quality of my work judged critically by supervisors, customers, or others

Frontiers of Knowledge	Working in one of the physical sciences or human research; or working in a company that is technically excellent and striving for product advances
Influence	Changing others' attitudes or modifying their opinions, convincing them to do something or purchase something
Competition	Engaging in activities that pit my abilities against others' where there are clear win-and-lose outcomes
Time Freedom	Pursuing responsibilities according to my own schedule; no specific work hours required
Collegiality	Having close working relationships with a group; working as a team toward common goals
Competence	Working in those areas in which I feel I have talents and can excel
Leisure	Having enough time for leisure pursuits; no significant overtime required
Friendships	Developing close personal relationships with people as a result of my work activities
Challenge	Stretching myself with new, unique, or difficult issues to resolve
Precision	Working in situations in which there is little tolerance for error
Helping Others	Providing services or assistance to other people in a direct way, either individually or in small groups

You will also need to make five "category cards," labeled with these categories:

Always Valued
Often Valued
Sometimes Valued
Seldom Valued
Never Valued

Instructions

The purpose of this exercise is to identify the six to eight driving values that produce 90 percent of your behaviors under normal conditions. You will need the Values Card Deck that consists of five category cards and thirty-six values cards. This exercise should take approximately thirty minutes.

Step 1: Arrange the value category cards.

Lay out the five category cards on a flat surface in a horizontal line so that they read from the left to the right, "Always Valued," "Often Valued," "Sometimes Valued," "Seldom Valued," and "Never Valued." Think about what you value right now, today, this current period. This is not an exercise in what you believe you *should* value but what you actually do value in carrying out your tasks every day on the job. This will be situational in some cases, but will also reflect things you are committed to fairly consistently all the time. Values change slowly over time, reflecting both our personality and our circumstances.

Step 2: Sort the values cards.

Each values card lists the name of a value and has a short phrase that describes the meaning assigned to that value for this exercise. Sort the cards based on how you feel about them under one of the category cards. Do not spend too much time contemplating what ranking you want to assign each value. Go with your first response. You will end up with a long column of cards under some categories and a shorter column under others. This is natural.

Step 3: Prioritizing.

Look first at the "Always Valued" cards. Sort them in order of priority, the one that is most important to you at the top, least important at the bottom. Once this is done set the top eight cards aside. You may return all the other cards to the deck.

WHAT IF I have too many cards in the "Always Valued" category to prioritize them easily? In this case, lay out the category cards "Always Valued," "Often Valued," and "Sometimes Valued" in the same manner as step 1 and resort the cards you originally put in "Always Valued" under these three categories (repeating steps 1 and 2).

WHAT IF I have fewer than eight cards in the "Always Valued" category? In this case take all the cards from the "Always Valued" and "Sometimes Valued" categories, set the rest aside, and resort these cards under all five categories until you have at least eight cards under "Always Valued." Now prioritize these cards.

Step 4: Record your team's top six to eight driving values.

In order to determine the team's set of driving values, make a list of each value that is shared by at least three people on the team. If this list includes more than eight values, make a new list of each value that is shared by at least four people on the team. Repeat this process until you have a list of six to eight values. In any effort the team is engaged in together, these driving values will produce most of the *team behavior* you see. If you cannot come up with a consensus of six to eight driving values for the team, you can assume that there are none.

Repeat the card sort exercise, asking each team member to sort their card decks in the same way but answering the question "What does the *team* need in order to accomplish its objectives, goals, and tasks?" This exercise is *not* about what each individual prefers or believes to be true about himself or herself and will produce an initial consensus around the driving values the work requires in the team's estimation. This list can be compared to the consensus list of values the team possesses in order to understand what needs to change.

Notice that this group exercise assumes some degree of planning has already taken place. There needs to be some agreement on mission (or vision or aim) as well as a few clear goals, objectives, and tasks already identified for the exercise to be meaningful. This doesn't mean you must have completed a full-blown strategic and cultural ministry planning process (though this would be ideal and actually is an element in the planning process as we currently teach it).

Plans always change. You are doing well if you hit your target one-third of the time, exceed your target one-third of the time, and miss your target one-third of the time. For this reason it is always important to revisit your plans and then go through the team version of the values card sort exercise again to ensure you have the right people doing the right things at the right time. We also offer *Vocational Fit* and *Team Design* resources and facilitations for ministries. These interactive workshops focus on purpose, spiritual gifts, values, design, and obstacles to overcome in helping teams prepare to plan together; incorporating calling, best use, motivation, skills, and success into the process.